ROWAN

Winter Kids

20 designs for boys & girls aged 3 to 12 years

Mia
by Lisa Richardson
Felted Tweed
Pattern Page 72

Harry

by Lisa Richardson
Wool Cotton
Pattern Page 63

Olivia
by Marie Wallin
Felted Tweed
Pattern Page 74

Charlie Snood
by Lisa Richardson
Cocoon
Pattern Page 82

Tobias
by Grace Melville
British Sheep Breeds DK
Pattern Page 83

Billy
by Marie Wallin
Pure Wool DK
Pattern Page 49

Betty
by Marie Wallin
Pure Wool 4 ply
Pattern Page 47

Ava
by Lisa Richardson
Colourscape Chunky
Pattern Page 46

14

Frances
by Lisa Richardson
Felted Tweed
Pattern Page 59

Jacob
by Lisa Richardson
Felted Tweed Chunky & Colourscape Chunky
Pattern Page 68

Imogen
by Grace Melville
Cocoon
Pattern Page 66

Elsie
by Marie Wallin
Felted Tweed
Pattern Page 56

Ethan

by Marie Wallin
Colourscape Chunky
Pattern Page 58

2

Doris
by Marie Wallin
British Sheep Breeds DK
Pattern Page 54

Doris
by Marie Wallin
British Sheep Breeds DK
Pattern Page 54

Ella
by Marie Wallin
Wool Cotton
Pattern Page 81

Charlie Snood
by Lisa Richardson
Cocoon
Pattern Page 82

Bunny

by Marie Wallin
British Sheep Breeds DK
Pattern Page 51

Mabel

by Marie Wallin
Cocoon
Pattern Page 70

Harry
by Lisa Richardson
Wool Cotton
Pattern Page 63

Alfie
by Lisa Richardson
Pure Wool 4 ply
Pattern Page 44

41

Gallery

Mia
Image Page 2
Pattern Page 72

Harry (1st colourway)
Image Page 4
Pattern Page 63

Olivia
Image Page 7
Pattern Page 74

Tobias & Charlie Snood
Image Page 8 & 9
Pattern Page Tobias 83
Pattern Page Charlie Snood 82

Billy
Image Page 10
Pattern Page 49

Betty
Image Page 12
Pattern Page 47

Ava
Image Page 14
Pattern Page 46

Frances
Image Page 16
Pattern Page 59

Jacob
Image Page 18
Pattern Page 68

Imogen
Image Page 21
Pattern Page 66

Elsie
Image Page 22
Pattern Page 56

Ethan
Image Page 25
Pattern Page 58

Doris (shade 784)
Image Page 26
Pattern Page 54

Doris (shade 782)
Image Page 28
Pattern Page 54

Reggie
Image Page 30
Pattern Page 79

Ella
Image Page 33
Pattern Page 81

Grace & Bunny
Image Page 34
Pattern Page Grace 60
Pattern Page Bunny 51

Mabel
Image Page 36
Pattern Page 70

Harry (2nd colourway)
Image Page 39
Pattern Page 63

Alfie
Image Page 41
Pattern Page 44

Alfie ❖ ❖ ❖

By Lisa Richardson

Main Image Page 41

SIZE

To fit age

| 3-4 | 5-6 | 7-8 | 9-10 | 11-12 | years |

YARN

Rowan Pure Wool 4 ply

A Mocha 417

2	2	2	2	3	x 50gm

B Eau de Nil 450

1	1	1	1	1	x 50gm

C Avocado 419

1	1	1	1	1	x 50gm

D Toffee 453

1	1	1	1	1	x 50gm

E Quarry Tile 457

1	1	1	1	1	x 50gm

F Havana 458

1	1	1	1	1	x 50gm

NEEDLES

1 pair 2¾mm (no 12) (US 2) needles
1 pair 3¼mm (no 10) (US 3) needles
2¾mm (no 12) (US 2) circular needle

TENSION

30 sts and 29 rows to 10 cm measured over patterned st st using 3¼mm (US 3) needles.

BACK

Using 2¾mm (US 2) needles and yarn A cast on 98 [106: 110: 118: 122] sts.
Row 1 (RS): K2, ★P2, K2, rep from ★ to end.
Row 2: P2, ★K2, P2, rep from ★ to end.
These 2 rows form rib.
Joining in and breaking off colours as required, cont in rib in stripes as folls:
Rows 3 and 4: Using yarn B.
Rows 5 and 6: Using yarn C.
Rows 7 and 8: Using yarn D.
Rows 9 and 10: Using yarn E.
Rows 11 and 12: Using yarn F.
Rows 13 and 14: Using yarn A.
Rows 15 and 16: Using yarn B.
Rows 17 and 18: Using yarn C and inc [dec: inc: dec: inc] 1 st at end

of last row. 99 [105: 111: 117: 123] sts.
Change to 3¼mm (US 3) needles.
Beg and ending rows as indicated, using the **fairisle** technique as described on the information page and repeating the 24 row patt rep throughout, now work in patt from chart, which is worked entirely in st st beg with a K row, as folls:
Cont straight until back meas 22 [23: 24: 25: 26] cm, ending with RS facing for next row.
Shape armholes
Keeping patt correct, cast off 5 [5: 4: 4: 3] sts at beg of next 2 rows.
89 [95: 103: 109: 117] sts.★★
Dec 1 st at each end of next 5 rows, then on foll 6 [5: 4: 3: 2] alt rows.
67 [75: 85: 93: 103] sts.
Cont straight until armhole meas 14 [15: 16: 17: 18] cm, ending with RS facing for next row.
Shape shoulders and back neck
Cast off 4 [4: 6: 6: 8] sts at beg of next 2 rows. 59 [67: 73: 81: 87] sts.
Next row (RS): Cast off 4 [4: 6: 6: 8] sts, patt until there are 6 [8: 8: 10: 11] sts on right needle and turn, leaving rem sts on a holder.
Work each side of neck separately.
Cast off 3 sts at beg of next row.
Cast off rem 3 [5: 5: 7: 8] sts.
With RS facing, rejoin appropriate yarns to rem sts, cast off centre 39 [43: 45: 49: 49] sts, patt to end.
Complete to match first side, reversing shapings.

FRONT

Work as given for back to ★★.
Dec 1 st at each end of next 5 rows, then on foll 1 [2: 3: 3: 2] alt rows.
77 [81: 87: 93: 103] sts.
Work 1 [1: 1: 3: 7] rows, ending with RS facing for next row.
Divide for neck
Next row (RS): (K2tog) 1 [1: 1: 0: 0] times, patt 36 [38: 41: 46: 51] sts and turn, leaving rem sts on a holder.
Work each side of neck separately.
Keeping patt correct, dec 1 st at neck edge of next 20 [22: 24: 26: 26] rows, then on foll 2 [2: 1: 1: 1] alt rows **and at same time** dec 1 st at armhole edge of 2nd [2nd: 0: 0: 0] and foll 3 [1: 0: 0: 0] alt rows.
11 [13: 17: 19: 24] sts.
Cont straight until front matches back to beg of shoulder shaping, ending with RS facing for next row.
Shape shoulder
Cast off 4 [4: 6: 6: 8] sts at beg of next and foll alt row.

Work 1 row.

Cast off rem 3 [5: 5: 7: 8] sts.

With RS facing, slip centre st onto a holder, rejoin appropriate yarns to rem sts, patt to last 2 [2: 2: 0: 0] sts, (K2tog) 1 [1: 1: 0: 0] times. 37 [39: 42: 46: 51] sts.

Complete to match first side, reversing shapings.

MAKING UP

Press as described on the information page.

Join both shoulder seams using back stitch, or mattress stitch if preferred.

Neckband

With RS facing, using 2¾mm (US 2) circular needle and yarn E, pick up and knit 38 [38: 42: 42: 42] sts down left side of neck, K st on holder at base of V and mark this st with a coloured thread, pick up and knit 38 [38: 42: 42: 42] sts up right side of neck, then 46 [50: 54: 58: 58] sts from back. 123 [127: 139: 143: 143] sts.

Round 1 (RS): ★K2, P2, rep from ★ to within 2 sts of marked st, K1, sl next 2 sts as though to K2tog (marked st is 2nd of these 2 sts), K1, pass 2 slipped sts over, K1, P2, ★★K2, P2, rep from ★★ to end.

This round sets position of rib.

Keeping rib correct and joining in and breaking off colours as required, cont as folls:

Round 2: Using yarn D, rib to within 1 st of marked st, sl next 2 sts as though to K2tog (marked st is 2nd of these 2 sts), K1, pass 2 slipped sts over, rib to end.

Round 3: As round 2.

Rounds 4 and 5: As round 2 but using yarn C.

Rounds 6 and 7: As round 2 but using yarn B.

Round 8: As round 2 but using yarn A. 107 [111: 123: 127: 127] sts.

Using yarn A, cast off in rib, still decreasing 1 st either side of marked st as before.

Armhole borders (both alike)

With RS facing, using 2¾mm (US 2) needles and yarn E, pick up and knit 98 [102: 110: 114: 118] sts evenly all round armhole edge.

Beg with row 2, work in rib as given for back, working in stripes as folls:

Row 1: Using yarn E.

Rows 2 and 3: Using yarn D.

Rows 4 and 5: Using yarn C.

Rows 6 and 7: Using yarn B.

Row 8: Using yarn A.

Using yarn A, cast off in rib (on **WS**).

See information page for finishing instructions.

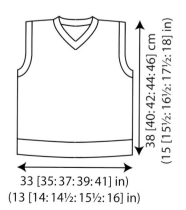

38 [40: 42: 44: 46] cm
(15 [15½: 16½: 17½: 18] in)

33 [35: 37: 39: 41] in)
(13 [14: 14½: 15½: 16] in)

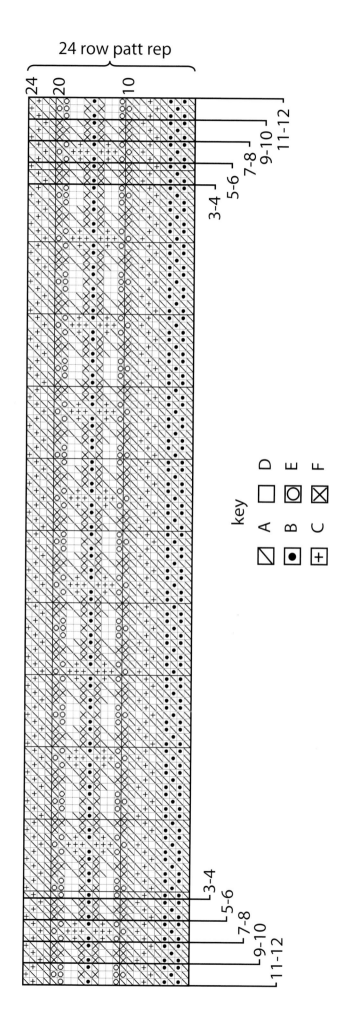

24 row patt rep

24 20 10

11-12
9-10
7-8
5-6
3-4

3-4
5-6
7-8
9-10
11-12

key

A D
B E
C F

Main Image Page 14

Ava ❖

By Lisa Richardson

SIZE
To fit age

| 3-4 | 5-6 | 7-8 | 9-10 | 11-12 | years |

YARN
Rowan Colourscape Chunky

| 3 | 3 | 3 | 3 | 4 | x 100gm |

(photographed in Jungle 447)

NEEDLES
1 pair 7mm (no 2) (US 10½) needles

BUTTONS - 2 x BN1368 from Bedecked. Please see credits page for contact details.

TENSION
13 sts and 26 rows to 10 cm measured over g st using 7mm (US 10½) needles.

BODY (worked in one piece, beg at back hem edge)
Using 7mm (US 10½) needles cast on 45 [47: 51: 53: 55] sts.
Work in g st for 30 [34: 36: 38: 40] rows, ending with RS facing for next row.

Shape for sleeves
Inc 1 st at each end of next and foll 2 alt rows, then on foll row, ending with RS facing for next row. 53 [55: 59: 61: 63] sts.
Cast on 3 [3: 4: 4: 4] sts at beg of next 8 [4: 10: 6: 2] rows, then 4 [4: 0: 5: 5] sts at beg of foll 2 [6: 0: 4: 8] rows. 85 [91: 99: 105: 111] sts.
Work 26 [28: 30: 34: 36] rows, ending with RS facing for next row.

Divide for back neck
Next row (RS): K36 [38: 42: 44: 47] and turn, leaving rem sts on a holder.
Work on this set of sts only for right shoulder and front.
Dec 1 st at neck edge of next 4 rows. 32 [34: 38: 40: 43] sts.
Work 1 row, ending with RS facing for next row.
Place markers at both ends of last row to denote shoulder line.

Shape right front
Work 2 rows, ending with RS facing for next row.
Inc 1 st at neck edge of next 5 [5: 5: 7: 7] rows, ending with **WS** facing for next row. 37 [39: 43: 47: 50] sts.
Cast on 15 [17: 17: 17: 17] sts at beg of next row. 52 [56: 60: 64: 67] sts.
Work 3 rows, ending with **WS** facing for next row.
Next row (WS): K2, K2tog, yfwd (to make first buttonhole), K10 [12: 12: 14: 14], K2tog, yfwd (to make 2nd buttonhole), K to end.
Work 6 rows, ending with RS facing for next row.

Shape front opening edge
Next row (RS): K to last 3 sts, K2tog, K1.
Working all front opening edge decreases 1 st in from front opening edge as set by last row, dec 1 st at end of 10th and 0 [0: 1: 1: 1] foll 8th row. 50 [54: 57: 61: 64] sts.
Work 5 [7: 1: 3: 5] rows, ending with RS facing for next row.

Shape sleeve
Cast off 4 [4: 4: 5: 5] sts at beg of next and foll 0 [2: 4: 1: 3] alt rows, then 3 [3: 0: 4: 4] sts at beg of foll 4 [2: 0: 3: 1] alt rows **and at same time** dec 1 st at front slope edge on 3rd [next: 7th: 5th: 3rd] and foll 0 [8th: 0: 0: 6th] row. 33 [34: 36: 38: 38] sts.
Dec 1 st at side seam edge of next 2 rows, then on foll 2 alt rows **and at same time** dec 1 st at front opening edge of 2nd [6th: 4th: 2nd: 4th] and foll 0 [0: 0: 4th: alt] row. 28 [29: 31: 32: 32] sts.
Dec 1 st at front opening edge **only** on 2nd [4th: 2nd: 2nd: 2nd] and 1 [0: 0: 0: 0] foll 4th row, then on foll 7 [11: 15: 16: 18] alt rows, then on foll 9 [7: 3: 3: 1] rows, ending with RS facing for next row.
Cast off rem 10 [10: 12: 12: 12] sts.
With RS facing, rejoin yarn to rem sts, cast off centre 13 [15: 15: 17: 17] sts, K to end. 36 [38: 42: 44: 47] sts.
Complete to match right shoulder and front, reversing shapings and omitting buttonholes.

MAKING UP
Press as described on the information page.

Neckband
With RS facing and using 7mm (US 10½) needles, beg and ending at front opening edges, pick up and knit 21 [23: 23: 25: 25] sts up right side of neck to shoulder line marker, 23 [25: 25: 27: 27] sts from back to other shoulder line marker, then 21 [23: 23: 25: 25] sts down left side of neck. 65 [71: 71: 77: 77] sts.
Cast off knitwise (on **WS**).
See information page for finishing instructions.

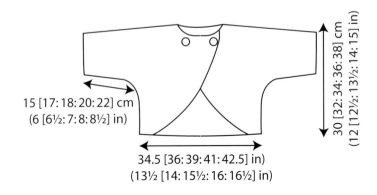

15 [17: 18: 20: 22] cm
(6 [6½: 7: 8: 8½] in)

34.5 [36: 39: 41: 42.5] in)
(13½ [14: 15½: 16: 16½] in)

30 [32: 34: 36: 38] cm
(12 [12½: 13½: 14: 15] in)

Main Image Page 12

Betty
By Marie Wallin

YARN

To fit age

| 3-4 | 5-6 | 7-8 | 9-10 | 11-12 | years |

Rowan Pure Wool 4 ply

| 5 | 6 | 6 | 7 | 8 | x 50gm |

(photographed in Raspberry 428)

NEEDLES

1 pair 3¼mm (no 10) (US 3) needles
2¾mm (no 12) (US 2) circular needle

BUTTONS – 1 x BN1367 (15mm) from Bedecked. Please see credits page for contact details.

TENSION

30 sts and 34 rows to 10 cm measured over main patt, 28 sts and 36 rows to 10 cm measured over sleeve patt, both using 3¼mm (US 3) needles.

BACK

Using 3¼mm (US 3) needles cast on 110 [116: 122: 128: 134] sts.
Work in main patt as folls:
Row 1 (WS): Purl.
Row 2: K2 [0: 3: 2: 0], (K2tog, K2, yfwd, K1) 0 [1: 1: 0: 1] times, ★yfwd, K2, sl 1, K1, psso, K2tog, K2, yfwd, K1, rep from ★ to last 0 [3: 6: 0: 3] sts, (yfwd, K2, sl 1, K1, psso) 0 [0: 1: 0: 0] times, K0 [3: 2: 0: 3].
Row 3: Purl.
Row 4: K1 [4: 2: 1: 4], (K2tog, K2, yfwd, K1) 0 [0: 1: 0: 0] times, ★yfwd, K2, sl 1, K1, psso, K2tog, K2, yfwd, K1, rep from ★ to last 1 [4: 7: 1: 4] sts, (yfwd, K2, sl 1, K1, psso) 0 [1: 1: 0: 1] times, K1 [0: 3: 1: 0].
These 4 rows form main patt.
Cont in patt, shaping side seams by dec 1 st at each end of 12th and 4 foll 14th rows. 100 [106: 112: 118: 124] sts.
Cont straight until back meas 27 [28: 29: 30: 31] cm, ending with RS facing for next row.
Shape armholes
Keeping patt correct, cast off 3 sts at beg of next 2 rows. 94 [100: 106: 112: 118] sts.
Dec 1 st at each end of next 7 [5: 5: 3: 3] rows, then on foll 4 [4: 3: 3: 2] alt rows. 72 [82: 90: 100: 108] sts.★★
Cont straight until armhole meas 13 [14: 15: 16: 17] cm, ending with RS facing for next row.
Shape shoulders and back neck
Cast off 5 [6: 7: 8: 9] sts at beg of next 2 rows. 62 [70: 76: 84: 90] sts.
Next row (RS): Cast off 5 [6: 7: 8: 9] sts, patt until there are 9 [10: 11: 12: 14] sts on right needle and turn, leaving rem sts on a holder.

Work each side of neck separately.
Cast off 4 sts at beg of next row.
Cast off rem 5 [6: 7: 8: 10] sts.
With RS facing, rejoin yarn to rem sts, cast off centre 34 [38: 40: 44: 44] sts, patt to end.
Complete to match first side, reversing shapings.

FRONT
Work as given for neck to ★★.
Work 1 [5: 11: 15: 19] rows, ending with RS facing for next row.
Divide for front opening
Next row (RS): Patt 32 [37: 41: 46: 50] sts, K2, K2tog and turn, leaving rem sts on a holder.
Work each side of neck separately.
Next row (WS): K1, P to end.
Next row: Patt to last 3 sts, K1, K2tog.
Next row: K1, P to end.
Next row: Patt to last 2 sts, K2tog. 33 [38: 42: 47: 51] sts.
Next row: K1, P to end.
Next row: Patt to last st, K1.
Rep last 2 rows until 16 [16: 16: 18: 18] rows less have been worked than on back to beg of shoulder shaping, ending with RS facing for next row.
Next row (RS): Patt to last st, M1, K1.
Next row: K1, P to end.
Next row: Patt to last 2 sts, K1, M1, K1.
Next row: K1, P to end.
Next row: Patt to last 3 sts, K2, M1, K1. 36 [41: 45: 50: 54] sts.
Next row: K1, P to end.
Shape neck
Next row (RS): Patt 23 [26: 29: 33: 37] sts and turn, leaving rem 13 [15: 16: 17: 17] sts on another holder.
Keeping patt correct, dec 1 st at neck edge of next 6 rows, then on foll 1 [1: 1: 2: 2] alt rows. 16 [19: 22: 25: 29] sts.
Work 1 row, ending with RS facing for next row.
Shape shoulder
Cast off 5 [6: 7: 8: 9] sts at beg of next and foll alt row **and at same time** dec 1 st at neck edge of next row.
Work 1 row.
Cast off rem 5 [6: 7: 8: 10] sts.
With RS facing, rejoin yarn to rem sts on first holder, K2tog, K2, patt to end. 35 [40: 44: 49: 53] sts.
Next row (WS): P to last st, K1.
Next row: K2tog, K1, patt to end.
Next row: P to last st, K1.

Next row: K2tog, patt to end. 33 [38: 42: 47: 51] sts.

Next row: P to last st, K1.

Next row: K1, patt to end.

Rep last 2 rows until 16 [16: 16: 18: 18] rows less have been worked than on back to beg of shoulder shaping, ending with RS facing for next row.

Next row (RS): K1, M1, patt to end.

Next row: P to last st, K1.

Next row: K1, M1, K1, patt to end.

Next row: P to last st, K1.

Next row: K1, M1, K2, patt to end. 36 [41: 45: 50: 54] sts.

Next row: P to last st, K1.

Shape neck

Next row (RS): Patt 13 [15: 16: 17: 17] sts and slip these sts onto another holder, patt to end. 23 [26: 29: 33: 37] sts.

Complete to match first side, reversing shaping.

SLEEVES

Lower sleeve

Using 3¼mm (US 3) needles cast on 54 [56: 60: 64: 68] sts.

Work in main patt as folls:

Row 1 (WS): Purl.

Row 2: K0 [1: 3: 1: 3], (K2tog, K2, yfwd) 0 [0: 0: 1: 1] times, ★K1, yfwd, K2, sl 1, K1, psso, K2tog, K2, yfwd, rep from ★ to last 9 [1: 3: 5: 7] sts, (K1, yfwd, K2, sl 1, K1, psso) 1 [0: 0: 1: 1] times, K4 [1: 3: 0: 2].

Row 3: Purl.

Row 4: K4 [1: 3: 0: 2], (K2tog, K2, yfwd, K1) 1 [0: 0: 1: 1] times, ★yfwd, K2, sl 1, K1, psso, K2tog, K2, yfwd, K1, rep from ★ to last 0 [1: 3: 5: 7] sts, (yfwd, K2, sl 1, K1, psso) 0 [0: 0: 1: 1] times, K0 [1: 3: 1: 3].

These 4 rows form main patt.

Cont in patt, shaping sides by inc 1 st at each end of 2nd [2nd: 2nd: 2nd: 4th] and 3 [4: 1: 3: 0] foll 8th rows, then on 0 [0: 3: 2: 4] foll 10th rows, taking inc sts into st st until there are sufficient to take into patt. 62 [66: 70: 76: 78] sts.

Work 6 [4: 2: 0: 6] rows, ending with **WS** facing for next row.

Next row (WS): P30 [10: 11: 7: 6] , P2tog, (P- [20: 21: 13: 14], P2tog) 0 [2: 2: 4: 4] times, P30 [10: 11: 7: 6]. 61 [63: 67: 71: 73] sts.

Break yarn and leave these sts on a holder.

Upper sleeve

Using 3¼mm (US 3) needles cast on 81 [84: 89: 94: 97] sts.

Work in g st for 2 rows, ending with RS facing for next row.

Beg with a K row, work in st st for 5 rows, ending with **WS** facing for next row.

Next row (WS): P1 [0: 1: 1: 1], (P1, P2tog, P1) 20 [21: 22: 23: 24] times, P0 [0: 0: 1: 0]. 61 [63: 67: 71: 73] sts.

Join sections

Holding WS of upper sleeve against RS of lower sleeve, K tog first st of upper sleeve with first st of lower sleeve, ★K tog next st of upper sleeve with next st of lower sleeve, rep from ★ to end. 61 [63: 67: 71: 73] sts.

Next row (WS): Purl.

Now work in sleeve patt as folls:

Row 1 (RS): (Inc in first st) 0 [1: 0: 0: 1] times, K to last 0 [1: 0: 0: 1] st, (inc in last st) 0 [1: 0: 0: 1] times. 61 [65: 67: 71: 75] sts.

Row 2 and every foll alt row: Purl.

Row 3: K0 [2: 3: 2: 4], (yfwd, sl 1, K2tog, psso, yfwd) 0 [0: 0: 1: 1] times, ★K5, yfwd, sl 1, K2tog, psso, yfwd, rep from ★ to last 5 [7: 8: 2: 4] sts, K5 [7: 8: 2: 4].

Row 5: (Inc in first st) 0 [0: 1: 0: 0] times, K0 [2: 2: 3: 5], (yfwd, sl 1, K1, psso) 0 [0: 0: 1: 1] times, ★K6, yfwd, sl 1, K1, psso, rep from ★ to last 5 [7: 8: 2: 4] sts, K5 [7: 7: 2: 4], (inc in last st) 0 [0: 1: 0: 0] times. 61 [65: 69: 71: 75] sts.

Row 7: (Inc in first st) 0 [0: 0: 1: 0] times, K to last 0 [0: 0: 1: 0] st, (inc in last st) 0 [0: 0: 1: 0] times. 61 [65: 69: 73: 75] sts.

Row 9: (Inc in first st) 1 [0: 0: 0: 0] times, (yfwd, sl 1, K2tog, psso, yfwd) 1 [0: 0: 0: 0] times, K4 [2: 4: 6: 7], ★K1, yfwd, sl 1, K2tog, psso, yfwd, K4, rep from ★ to last 5 [7: 1: 3: 4] sts, (K1, yfwd, sl 1, K2tog, psso, yfwd) 1 [1: 0: 0: 0] times, K0 [3: 1: 3: 4], (inc in last st) 1 [0: 0: 0: 0] times. 63 [65: 69: 73: 75] sts.

Row 11: (Inc in first st) 0 [1: 0: 0: 1] times, K1 [1: 4: 6: 6], ★K2, yfwd, sl 1, K1, psso, K4, rep from ★ to last 6 [7: 1: 3: 4] sts, (K2, yfwd, sl 1, K1, psso) 1 [1: 0: 0: 0] times, K2 [2: 1: 3: 3], (inc in last st) 0 [1: 0: 0: 1] times. 63 [67: 69: 73: 77] sts.

Row 12: Purl.

These 12 rows form sleeve patt and cont sleeve shaping.

Cont in patt, shaping sides by inc 1 st at each end of 7th [9th: 3rd: 5th: 9th] and every foll 10th row until there are 73 [77: 81: 85: 89] sts, taking inc sts into patt.

Cont straight until sleeve meas 32 [36: 40: 44: 48] cm **from cast-on edge of lower sleeve**, ending with RS facing for next row.

Shape top

Keeping patt correct, cast off 3 sts at beg of next 2 rows. 67 [71: 75: 79: 83] sts.

Dec 1 st at each end of next 5 rows, then on every foll alt row to 51 sts, then on foll 7 rows, ending with RS facing for next row. 37 sts.

Cast off 4 sts at beg of next 4 rows.

Cast off rem 21 sts.

MAKING UP

Press as described on the information page.

Join both shoulder seams using back stitch, or mattress stitch if preferred.

Neckband

With RS facing and using 2¾mm (US 2) circular needles, slip 13 [15: 16: 17: 17] sts from right front holder onto right needle, rejoin yarn and pick up and knit 10 [10: 10: 12: 12] sts up right side of neck, 39 [43: 45: 49: 49] sts from back, and 10 [10: 10: 12: 12] sts down left side of neck, then patt 13 [15: 16: 17: 17] sts from left front holder. 85 [93: 97: 107: 107] sts.

Row 1 (WS): Knit.

Row 2: K1, ★wrap yarn over right needle point by bringing yarn under needle and taking it back over needle, lift K st originally on right needle over this loop and off right needle, rep from ★ 5 times more (to form button loop), K to end.

Cast off knitwise (on **WS**).

See information page for finishing instructions, setting in sleeves using the set-in method.

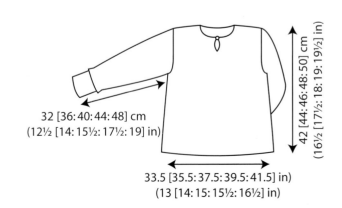

32 [36: 40: 44: 48] cm
(12½ [14: 15½: 17½: 19] in)

42 [44: 46: 48: 50] cm
(16½ [17½: 18: 19: 19½] in)

33.5 [35.5: 37.5: 39.5: 41.5] in)
(13 [14: 15: 15½: 16½] in)

Main Image Page 10

Billy
By Maria Wallin

YARN

To fit age

3-4	5-6	7-8		years

Rowan Pure Wool DK

A Clay 048

2	2	3	x 50gm

B Earth 018

1	1	2	x 50gm

C Ox blood 049

1	1	1	x 50gm

D Emerald 022

1	1	1	x 50gm

E Cypress 007

2	2	2	x 50gm

NEEDLES

1 pair 3¼mm (no 10) (US 3) needles
1 pair 4mm (no 8) (US 6) needles

BUTTONS - 6 x BN1367 (15mm) from Bedecked. Please see credits page for contact details.

TENSION

22 sts and 30 rows to 10 cm measured over st st using 4mm (US 6) needles.

STRIPE SEQUENCE

Rows 1 and 2: Using yarn A.
Rows 3 and 4: Using yarn B.
Rows 5 and 6: Using yarn A.
Rows 7 to 10: Using yarn B.
Rows 11 and 12: Using yarn A.
Rows 13 and 14: Using yarn B.
Rows 15 and 16: Using yarn A.
Rows 17 and 18: Using yarn C.
Rows 19 and 20: Using yarn A.
Rows 21 to 24: Using yarn C.
Rows 25 and 26: Using yarn A.
Rows 27 and 28: Using yarn C.
Rows 29 and 30: Using yarn A.
Rows 31 and 32: Using yarn D.
Rows 33 and 34: Using yarn A.
Rows 35 to 38: Using yarn D.
Rows 39 and 40: Using yarn A.
Rows 41 and 42: Using yarn D.
Rows 43 and 44: Using yarn A.
Rows 45 and 46: Using yarn E.
Rows 47 and 48: Using yarn A.
Rows 49 to 52: Using yarn E.
Rows 53 and 54: Using yarn A.
Rows 55 and 56: Using yarn E.
These 56 rows form stripe sequence and are repeated.

BACK

Using 3¼mm (US 3) needles and yarn E cast on 78 [82: 90] sts.
Row 1 (RS): K2, *P2, K2, rep from * to end.
Row 2: P2, *K2, P2, rep from * to end.
These 2 rows form rib.
Work in rib for a further 14 rows, inc [inc: dec] 1 st at end of last row and ending with RS facing for next row. 79 [83: 89] sts.
Change to 4mm (US 6) needles.
Beg with stripe row 1 and a K row, now work in st st in stripe sequence (see above) as folls:
Cont straight until back meas 26 [27: 28] cm, ending with RS facing for next row.

Shape armholes

Keeping stripes correct, cast off 5 sts at beg of next 2 rows. 69 [73: 79] sts.
Dec 1 st at each end of next and foll 5 alt rows. 57 [61: 67] sts.
Cont straight until armhole meas 13 [14: 15] cm, ending with RS facing for next row.

Shape shoulders and back neck

Cast off 4 [5: 5] sts at beg of next 2 rows. 49 [51: 57] sts.
Next row (RS): Cast off 4 [5: 5] sts, K until there are 8 [7: 9] sts on right needle and turn, leaving rem sts on a holder.
Work each side of neck separately.
Cast off 3 sts at beg of next row.
Cast off rem 5 [4: 6] sts.
With RS facing, rejoin appropriate yarns to rem sts, cast off centre 25 [27: 29] sts, K to end.
Complete to match first side, reversing shapings.

LEFT FRONT

Using 3¼mm (US 3) needles and yarn E cast on 39 [39: 43] sts.
Row 1 (RS): K2, *P2, K2, rep from * to last st, K1.
Row 2: K1, P2, *K2, P2, rep from * to end.
These 2 rows form rib.
Work in rib for a further 14 rows, inc 0 [2: 1] sts evenly across last row and ending with RS facing for next row. 39 [41: 44] sts.
Change to 4mm (US 6) needles.
Beg with stripe row 1 and a K row, now work in st st in stripe sequence

(see previus page) as folls:

Cont straight until left front matches back to beg of armhole shaping, ending with RS facing for next row.

Shape armhole

Keeping stripes correct, cast off 5 sts at beg of next row. 34 [36: 39] sts.

Work 1 row.

Dec 1 st at armhole edge of next and foll alt row. 32 [34: 37] sts.

Work 1 row, ending with RS facing for next row.

Shape front slope

Keeping stripes correct, dec 1 st at end of next and foll 14 [15: 16] alt rows **and at same time** dec 1 st at armhole edge of next and foll 3 alt rows. 13 [14: 16] sts.

Cont straight until left front matches back to beg of shoulder shaping, ending with RS facing for next row.

Shape shoulder

Cast off 4 [5: 5] sts at beg of next and foll alt row.

Work 1 row.

Cast off rem 5 [4: 6] sts.

RIGHT FRONT

Using 3¼mm (US 3) needles and yarn E cast on 39 [39: 43] sts.

Row 1 (RS): K3, *P2, K2, rep from * to end.

Row 2: P2, *K2, P2, rep from * to last st, K1.

These 2 rows form rib.

Complete to match left front, reversing shapings.

SLEEVES

Using 3¼mm (US 3) needles and yarn D cast on 38 [42: 42] sts.

Work in rib as given for back for 12 rows, inc [dec: inc] 1 st at centre of last row and ending with RS facing for next row. 39 [41: 43] sts.

Change to 4mm (US 6) needles.

Beg with stripe row 1 and a K row, now work in st st in stripe sequence (see previous page) as folls:

Inc 1 st at each end of next and every foll 10th row to 53 [55: 57] sts, then on every foll 12th row until there are 55 [59: 63] sts.

Cont straight until sleeve meas 32 [36: 40] cm, ending with RS facing for next row.

Shape top

Keeping stripes correct, cast off 5 sts at beg of next 2 rows. 45 [49: 53] sts.

Dec 1 st at each end of next and foll 4 alt rows, then on foll row, ending with RS facing for next row.

Cast off rem 33 [37: 41] sts.

MAKING UP

Press as described on the information page.

Join both shoulder seams using back stitch, or mattress stitch if preferred. Mark centre back neck.

Right front band

With RS facing, using 3¼mm (US 3) needles and yarn C, beg at right front cast-on edge, pick up and knit 69 [74: 76] sts up right front opening edge to beg of front slope shaping, 38 [40: 45] sts up right front slope, then 16 [17: 18] sts to centre back neck. 123 [131: 139] sts.

Beg with row 2, work in rib as given for right front as folls:

For a girl

Work in rib for 3 rows, ending with RS facing for next row.

Row 4 (RS): Rib 3, yrn, work 2 tog (to make first buttonhole), rib 5, yrn, work 2 tog (to make 2nd buttonhole), *rib 12 [13: 14], yrn, work 2 tog (to make a buttonhole), rep from * 3 times more (6 buttonholes made), rib to end.

Work in rib for a further 3 rows, ending with RS facing for next row.

For a boy

Work in rib for 7 rows, ending with RS facing for next row.

For a girl or a boy

Cast off in rib.

Left front band

With RS facing, using 3¼mm (US 3) needles and yarn B, beg at centre back neck, pick up and knit 16 [17: 18] sts to shoulder seam, 38 [40: 45] sts down left front slope, then 69 [74: 76] sts down left front opening edge to cast-on edge. 123 [131: 139] sts.

Beg with row 2, work in rib as given for left front as folls:

For a girl

Work in rib for 7 rows, ending with RS facing for next row.

For a boy

Work in rib for 3 rows, ending with RS facing for next row.

Row 4 (RS): Rib to last 68 [72: 76] sts, *work 2 tog, yrn (to make a buttonhole), rib 12 [13: 14], rep from * 3 times more, work 2 tog, yrn (to make 5th buttonhole), rib 5, work 2 tog, yrn (to make 6th buttonhole), rib 3.

Work in rib for a further 3 rows, ending with RS facing for next row.

For a girl or a boy

Cast off in rib.

Join row-end edges of bands at centre back neck.

Elbow patches (make 2)

Using 4mm (US 6) needles and yarn E cast on 8 sts.

Row 1 (RS): Knit.

Row 2: K1, M1P, P6, M1P, K1.

Row 3: K1, M1, K8, M1, K1.

Row 4: K1, M1P, P10, M1P, K1. 14 sts.

Row 5: K1, M1, K to last st, M1, K1.

Row 6: K1, P to last st, K1.

Rep last 2 rows 1 [2: 3] times more. 18 [20: 22] sts.

Next row (RS): Knit.

Next row: K1, P to last st, K1.

Rep last 2 rows 7 times more.

Next row (RS): K1, K2tog, K to last 3 sts, K2tog tbl, K1.

Next row: K1, P to last st, K1.

Rep last 2 rows 0 [1: 2] times more. 16 sts.

Next row (RS): K1, K2tog, K10, K2tog tbl, K1.

Next row: K1, P2tog tbl, P8, P2tog, K1.

Next row: K1, K2tog, K6, K2tog tbl, K1.

Next row: K1, P2tog tbl, P4, P2tog, K1.

Cast off rem 8 sts.

Using photograph as a guide and yarn C, back stitch elbow patches in place onto sleeves.

See information page for finishing instructions, setting in sleeves using the shallow set-in method.

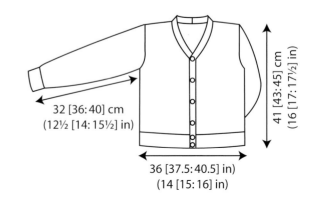

32 [36: 40] cm
(12½ [14: 15½] in)

41 [43: 45] cm
(16 [17: 17½] in)

36 [37.5: 40.5] in)
(14 [15: 16] in)

Bunny

By Marie Wallin

Main Image Page 34

SIZE
To fit age

| 7-8 | 9-10 | 11-12 | years |

YARN
Rowan British Sheep Breeds DK

A Mid Brown Bluefaced Leicester 782

| 4 | 5 | 5 | x 50gm |

B Brown Bluefaced Leicester 781

| 2 | 2 | 2 | x 50gm |

C Bluefaced Leicester 780

| 2 | 2 | 2 | x 50gm |

NEEDLES
1 pair 3¼mm (no 10) (US 3) needles
1 pair 4mm (no 8) (US 6) needles

BUTTONS - 2 x BN1367 (15mm) from Bedecked. Please see credits page for contact details.

TENSION
25 sts and 27 rows to 10 cm measured over patterned st st using 4mm (US 6) needles.

BACK
Using 3¼mm (US 3) needles and yarn A cast on 82 [86: 90] sts.
Row 1 (RS): K2, ★P2, K2, rep from ★ to end.
Row 2: P2, ★K2, P2, rep from ★ to end.
These 2 rows form rib.
Cont in rib until back meas 17 cm, ending with **WS** facing for next row.
Next row (WS): Rib 5 [1: 3], M1, (rib 6, M1) 12 [14: 14] times, rib 5 [1: 3]. 95 [101: 105] sts.
Change to 4mm (US 6) needles.
Beg and ending rows as indicated and using the **fairisle** technique as described on the information page, now work in patt from chart for body, which is worked entirely in st st beg with a K row, as folls:
Cont straight until chart row 22 [24: 28] has been completed, ending with RS facing for next row.
(Back should meas 25 [26: 27] cm.)
Shape raglan armholes
Keeping patt correct, cast off 3 sts at beg of next 2 rows. 89 [95: 99] sts.
Dec 1 st at each end of next 15 [13: 15] rows, then on foll 11 [14: 14] alt rows. 37 [41: 41] sts.
Work 1 row, ending after chart row 62 [68: 74] and with RS facing for next row.
Cast off.

FRONT
Work as given for back until 47 [53: 55] sts rem in raglan armhole shaping.
Work 1 row, ending after chart row 52 [56: 60] and with RS facing for next row.
Shape front neck
Next row (RS): K2tog, patt 7 [9: 11] sts and turn, leaving rem sts on a holder.
Work each side of neck separately. (**Note**: Front neck shaping is **NOT** shown on chart.)
Keeping patt correct, dec 1 st at neck edge of next 4 rows, then on foll 0 [1: 2] alt rows **and at same time** dec 1 st at raglan armhole edge of 2nd and foll 1 [2: 3] alt rows. 2 sts.
Work 1 row, ending with RS facing for next row.
Next row (RS): K2tog and fasten off.
With RS facing, rejoin yarns to rem sts, cast off centre 29 [31: 29] sts, patt to last 2 sts, K2tog. 8 [10: 12] sts.
Complete to match first side, reversing shapings.

SLEEVES
Using 3¼mm (US 3) needles and yarn A cast on 42 [46: 46] sts.
Work in rib as given for back, shaping sides by inc 1 st at each end of 9th and 0 [0: 4] foll 10th rows, then on 6 [6: 1] foll 8th rows, taking inc sts into rib. 56 [60: 58] sts.
Work 1 row, inc [dec: inc] 1 st at end of row and ending with RS facing for next row. 57 [59: 59] sts. (58 rows of rib completed.)
Change to 4mm (US 6) needles.
Beg and ending rows as indicated, beg with chart row 17 [7: 1] and using the **fairisle** technique as described on the information page, now work in patt from chart for sleeves, which is worked entirely in st st beg with a K row, as folls:
Inc 1 st at each end of 5th [7th: 7th] and 0 [2: 4] foll 8th rows, then on 6 [5: 4] foll 6th rows, then on 3 foll 4th rows, taking inc sts into patt. 77 [81: 83] sts.
Work 3 rows, ending after chart row 72 [74: 78] and with RS facing for next row.
Shape top
Keeping patt correct, cast off 3 sts at beg of next 2 rows. 71 [75: 77] sts.
Dec 1 st at each end of next 23 rows, then on every foll alt row until 15 sts rem.
Work 1 row, ending with RS facing for next row.
Left sleeve only
Dec 1 st at each end of next row, then cast off 4 sts at beg of foll row. 9 sts.
Dec 1 st at beg of next row, then cast off 4 sts at beg of foll row.
Right sleeve only
Cast off 5 sts at beg and dec 1 st at end of next row. 9 sts.

Work 1 row.
Cast off 4 sts at beg and dec 1 st at end of next row.
Work 1 row.
Both sleeves
Cast off rem 4 sts.

MAKING UP
Press as described on the information page.
Join both back raglan seams using back stitch, or mattress stitch if preferred.
Front neckband
With RS facing, using 3¼mm (US 3) needles and yarn A, pick up and knit 5 [7: 9] sts down left side of neck, 21 [23: 21] sts from front, then 5 [7: 9] sts up right side of neck. 31 [37: 39] sts.
Row 1 (WS): K1, ★P1, K1, rep from ★ to end.
Row 2: As row 1.
These 2 rows form moss st.
Work in moss st for 1 row more, ending with RS facing for next row.
Row 4 (RS): Moss st 3 sts, work 2 tog tbl, yrn (to make first buttonhole), moss st to last 5 sts, yrn, work 2 tog (to make 2nd buttonhole), moss st 3 sts.
Work in moss st for a further 3 rows, ending with RS facing for next row.

Cast off in moss st.
Back neckband
With RS facing, using 3¼mm (US 3) needles and yarn A, cast on 8 sts, turn and onto same needle pick up and knit 10 sts from top of right sleeve, 29 [33: 33] sts from back, and 10 sts from top of left sleeve, turn and cast on 8 sts. 65 [69: 69] sts.
Work in moss st as given for front neckband for 7 rows, ending with RS facing for next row.
Cast off in moss st.
Join front raglan seams below neckband sections. Attach buttons to ends of back neckband to correspond with buttonholes in front neckband.
See information page for finishing instructions.

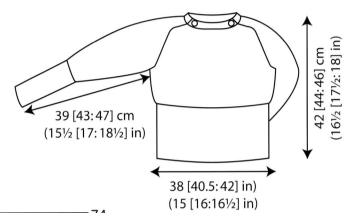

39 [43: 47] cm
(15½ [17: 18½] in)

42 [44: 46] cm
(16½ [17½: 18] in)

38 [40.5: 42] in)
(15 [16: 16½] in)

Body Chart

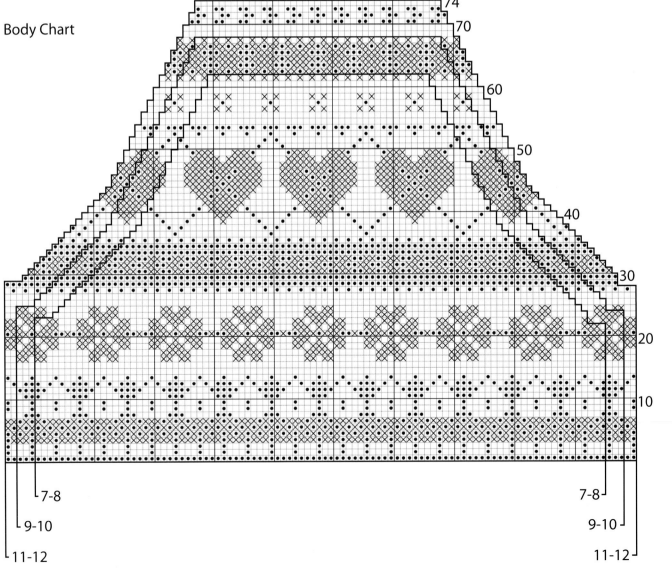

74
70
60
50
40
30
20
10

7-8
9-10
11-12

7-8
9-10
11-12

Sleeve Chart

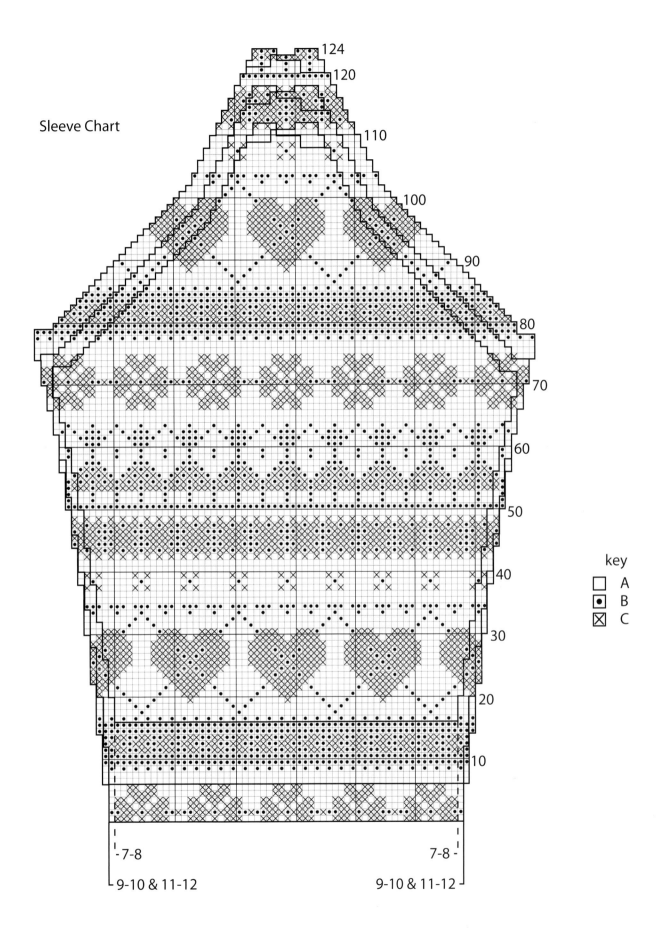

124
120
110
100
90
80
70
60
50
40
30
20
10

key
A
B
C

-7-8

7-8 -

9-10 & 11-12

9-10 & 11-12

Main Image Page 26 & 28

Doris ❖
By Marie Wallin

SIZE
To fit age

| 3-4 | 5-6 | 7-8 | 9-10 | 11-12 | years |

YARN
Rowan British Sheep Breeds DK

| 7 | 8 | 9 | 10 | 10 | x 50gm |

(photographed in Bluefaced Leicester Grey Suffolk 784 and Mid Brown Bluefaced Leicester 782)

NEEDLES
1 pair 4mm (no 8) (US 6) needles

BUTTONS – 1 x BN1367 (15mm) from Bedecked. Please see credits page for contact details.

RIBBON – 45 cm of 1 cm ribbon

TENSION
21 sts and 39 rows to 10 cm measured over moss st using 4mm (US 6) needles.

BACK
Using 4mm (US 6) needles cast on 75 [79: 83: 89: 93] sts.
Row 1 (RS): K1, ★P1, K1, rep from ★ to end.
Row 2: As row 1.
These 2 rows form moss st.
Cont in moss st, shaping side seams by dec 1 st at each end of 23rd and 3 foll 12th rows. 67 [71: 75: 81: 85] sts.
Cont straight until back meas 20 [21: 21: 21: 21] cm, ending with RS facing for next row.
Inc 1 st at each end of next and foll 10th [12th: 12th: 12th: 12th] row. 71 [75: 79: 85: 89] sts.
Cont straight until back meas 27 [28: 29: 30: 31] cm, ending with RS facing for next row.
Shape armholes
Cast off 3 sts at beg of next 2 rows. 65 [69: 73: 79: 83] sts.
Dec 1 st at each end of next 3 rows, then on foll 4 [3: 2: 2: 1] alt rows. 51 [57: 63: 69: 75] sts.

Cont straight until armhole meas 14 [15: 16: 17: 18] cm, ending with RS facing for next row.
Shape shoulders and back neck
Cast off 5 [6: 7: 8: 10] sts at beg of next 2 rows, then 6 [7: 8: 9: 10] sts at beg of foll 2 rows.
Cast off rem 29 [31: 33: 35: 35] sts.

LEFT FRONT
Using 4mm (US 6) needles cast on 71 [75: 79: 85: 89] sts.
Work in moss st as given for back, shaping side seam by dec 1 st at beg of 25th and 3 foll 12th rows. 67 [71: 75: 81: 85] sts.
Cont straight until left front meas 20 [21: 21: 21: 21] cm, ending with RS facing for next row.
Inc 1 st at beg of next and foll 10th [12th: 12th: 12th: 12th] row. 69 [73: 77: 83: 87] sts.
Cont straight until 12 rows less have been worked than on back to beg of armhole shaping, ending with RS facing for next row.
Shape front slope
Dec 1 st at end of next row and at same edge on foll 11 rows, ending with RS facing for next row. 57 [61: 65: 71: 75] sts.
Shape armhole
Cast off 3 sts at beg and dec 1 st at end of next row. 53 [57: 61: 67: 71] sts.
Dec 1 st at front slope edge of next row. 52 [56: 60: 66: 70] sts.
Dec 1 st at armhole edge of next 3 rows, then on foll 4 [3: 2: 2: 1] alt rows **and at same time** dec 1 st at front slope edge of next 11 [9: 7: 7: 5] rows. 34 [41: 48: 54: 61] sts.
Dec 1 st at front slope edge **only** on next 18 [22: 26: 30: 32] rows, then on foll 3 [4: 5: 5: 7] alt rows, then on 2 foll 4th rows. 11 [13: 15: 17: 20] sts.
Cont straight until left front matches back to beg of shoulder shaping, ending with RS facing for next row.
Shape shoulder
Cast off 5 [6: 7: 8: 10] sts at beg of next row.
Work 1 row.
Cast off rem 6 [7: 8: 9: 10] sts.

RIGHT FRONT
Using 4mm (US 6) needles cast on 71 [75: 79: 85: 89] sts.
Work in moss st as given for back, shaping side seam by dec 1 st

at end of 25th and 3 foll 12th rows. 67 [71: 75: 81: 85] sts.
Complete to match left front, reversing shapings.

SLEEVES

Using 4mm (US 6) needles cast on 39 [43: 45: 47: 49] sts.
Work in moss st as given for back, shaping sides by inc 1 st at each
end of 11th [13th: 15th: 17th: 19th] and every foll 12th [14th: 16th:
18th: 20th] row to 55 [47: 49: 51: 53] sts, then on every foll
14th [16th: 18th: 20th: 22nd] row until there are 57 [59: 61: 63: 65] sts.
Cont straight until sleeve meas 32 [36: 40: 44: 48] cm, ending with
RS facing for next row.

Shape top

Cast off 3 sts at beg of next 2 rows. 51 [53: 55: 57: 59] sts.
Dec 1 st at each end of next 3 rows, then on foll 2 alt rows, then
on 4 foll 4th rows. 33 [35: 37: 39: 41] sts.
Work 1 row.

Dec 1 st at each end of next and every foll alt row to 29 sts, then
on foll 9 rows, ending with RS facing for next row.
Cast off rem 11 sts.

MAKING UP

Press as described on the information page.
Join both shoulder seams using back stitch, or mattress stitch if
preferred.
See information page for finishing instructions, setting in sleeves
using the set-in method.
Cut ribbon into 2 equal lengths. Attach one length to right front
opening edge level with beg of front slope shaping and other
length to RS of left side seam 3 cm below underarm point. Make
a button loop on inside of right side seam 3 cm below underarm
point and attach button along left front opening edge level with
beg of front slope shaping.

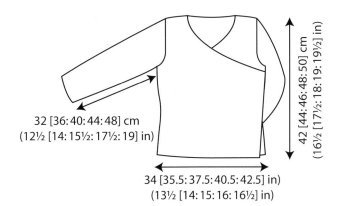

32 [36: 40: 44: 48] cm
(12½ [14: 15½: 17½: 19] in)

42 [44: 46: 48: 50] cm
(16½ [17½: 18: 19: 19½] in)

34 [35.5: 37.5: 40.5: 42.5] in)
(13½ [14: 15: 16: 16½] in)

Main Image Page 22

Elsie ❖ ❖

By Marie Wallin

YARN

To fit age

	3-4	5-6	7-8	9-10	years
Rowan Felted Tweed					
A Seasalter 178					
	1	2	2	2	x 50gm
B Paisley 171					
	1	1	1	2	x 50gm
C Bilberry 151					
	1	2	2	2	x 50gm
D Pine 158					
	1	1	1	2	x 50gm
E Ginger 154					
	1	1	2	2	x 50gm
F Avocado 161					
	1	1	1	2	x 50gm
G Gilt 160					
	1	2	2	2	x 50gm

NEEDLES

1 pair 3¼mm (no 10) (US 3) needles

TENSION

24 sts and 35 rows to 10 cm measured over st st, 31 sts and 35 rows to 10 cm measured over rib, both using 3¼mm (US 3) needles.

SKIRT STRIPE SEQUENCE

Rows 1 and 2: Using yarn B.
Rows 3 to 8: Using yarn C.
Rows 9 to 12: Using yarn D.
Rows 13 to 18: Using yarn E.
Rows 19 and 20: Using yarn F.
Rows 21 to 24: Using yarn G.
Rows 25 and 26: Using yarn A.
Rows 27 and 28: Using yarn D.
Rows 29 to 32: Using yarn F.
Rows 33 and 34: Using yarn B.
Rows 35 to 38: Using yarn C.
Rows 39 and 40: Using yarn E.
Rows 41 to 46: Using yarn G.
Rows 47 to 50: Using yarn A.
These 50 rows form skirt stripe sequence and are repeated.

RIB STRIPE SEQUENCE

Rows 1 and 2: Using yarn A.
Rows 3 and 4: Using yarn B.
Rows 5 and 6: Using yarn C.
Rows 7 and 8: Using yarn D.
Rows 9 and 10: Using yarn E.
Rows 11 and 12: Using yarn F.
Rows 13 and 14: Using yarn G.
These 14 rows form rib stripe sequence and are repeated.

BACK

Using 3¼mm (US 3) needles and yarn A cast on 99 [105: 111: 117] sts.
Row 1 (RS): K1, ★P1, K1, rep from ★ to end.
Row 2: As row 1.
These 2 rows form moss st.
Work in moss st for 1 row more, dec 1 st at end of row and ending with **WS** facing for next row. 98 [104: 110: 116] sts.
Beg with stripe row 1 and a P row, now work in st st in **skirt** stripe sequence (see above) as folls:
Cont straight until back meas 41 [44: 47: 50] cm, ending with RS facing for next row.
Beg with stripe row 1, now work in **rib** stripe sequence (see above) as folls:
Next row (RS): K0 [1: 0: 0], P0 [2: 2: 1], ★K2, P2, rep from ★ to last 2 [1: 0: 3] sts, K2 [1: 0: 2], P0 [0: 0: 1].
Next row: P0 [1: 0: 0], K0 [2: 2: 1], ★P2, K2, rep from ★ to last 2 [1: 0: 3] sts, P2 [1: 0: 2], K0 [0: 0: 1].
These 2 rows form rib.
Keeping **rib** stripe sequence correct, cont in rib, shaping side seams by inc 1 st at each end of 3rd and foll 10th [12th: 14th: 16th] row, taking inc sts into rib. 102 [108: 114: 120] sts.
Cont straight until back meas 47 [52: 57: 62] cm, ending with RS facing for next row.
Shape armholes
Keeping stripes correct, cast off 3 sts at beg of next 2 rows. 96 [102: 108: 114] sts.
Dec 1 st at each end of next 7 [5: 3: 3] rows, then on foll 4 [4: 4: 3] alt rows. 74 [84: 94: 102] sts.
Cont straight until armhole meas 13 [14: 15: 16] cm, ending with RS facing for next row.
Shape shoulders and back neck
Cast off 5 [6: 7: 8] sts at beg of next 2 rows. 64 [72: 80: 86] sts.
Next row (RS): Cast off 5 [6: 7: 8] sts, rib until there are 9 [11: 12: 13]

on right needle and turn, leaving rem sts on a holder.

Work each side of neck separately.

Cast off 4 sts at beg of next row.

Cast off rem 5 [7: 8: 9] sts.

With RS facing, rejoin appropriate yarns to rem sts, cast off centre 36 [38: 42: 44] sts, rib to end.

Complete to match first side, reversing shapings.

FRONT

Work as given for back until 16 [16: 16: 18] rows less have been worked than on back to beg of shoulder shaping, ending with RS facing for next row.

Shape neck

Next row (RS): Rib 27 [31: 34: 38] and turn, leaving rem sts on a holder.

Work each side of neck separately.

Keeping stripes correct, dec 1 st at neck edge of next 10 rows, then on foll 2 [2: 2: 3] alt rows. 15 [19: 22: 25] sts.

Work 1 row, ending with RS facing for next row.

Shape shoulder

Cast off 5 [6: 7: 8] sts at beg of next and foll alt row.

Work 1 row.

Cast off rem 5 [7: 8: 9] sts.

With RS facing, rejoin appropriate yarns to rem sts, cast off centre 20 [22: 26: 26] sts, rib to end.

Complete to match first side, reversing shapings.

SLEEVES

Using 3¼mm (US 3) needles and yarn A cast on 50 [54: 58: 62] sts.

Beg with stripe row 1, now work in **rib** stripe sequence (see above) as folls:

Row 1 (RS): K2, ★P2, K2, rep from ★ to end.

Row 2: P2, ★K2, P2, rep from ★ to end.

These 2 rows form rib.

Keeping **rib** stripe sequence correct, cont in rib, shaping sides by inc 1 st at each end of 3rd [3rd: 3rd: 5th] and every foll 6th [6th: 8th: 8th] row to 80 [70: 90: 82] sts, then on every foll 8th [8th: –: 10th] row until there are 82 [86: –: 94] sts, taking inc sts into rib.

Cont straight until sleeve meas 32 [36: 40: 44] cm, ending with RS facing for next row.

Shape top

Keeping stripes correct, cast off 3 sts at beg of next 2 rows. 76 [80: 84: 88] sts.

Dec 1 st at each end of next 7 rows, then on every foll alt row until 58 sts rem, then on foll 9 rows, ending with RS facing for next row. 40 sts.

Cast off 5 sts at beg of next 4 rows.

Cast off rem 20 sts.

MAKING UP

Press as described on the information page.

Join right seam using back stitch, or mattress stitch if preferred.

Neckband

With RS facing, using 3¼mm (US 3) needles and yarn A, pick up and knit 16 [16: 16: 18] sts down left side of neck, 15 [17: 19: 19] sts from front, 16 [16: 16: 18] sts up right side of neck, then 34 [36: 38: 40] sts from back. 81 [85: 89: 95] sts.

Work in moss st as given for back for 3 rows, ending with RS facing for next row.

Cast off in moss st.

See information page for finishing instructions, setting in sleeves using the set-in method.

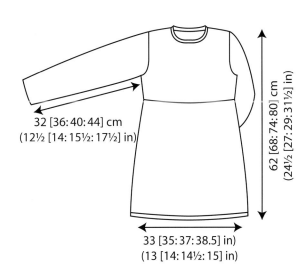

32 [36: 40: 44] cm
(12½ [14: 15½: 17½] in)

62 [68: 74: 80] cm
(24½ [27: 29: 31½] in)

33 [35: 37: 38.5] in)
(13 [14: 14½: 15] in)

Main Image Page 25

Ethan ❖
By Marie Wallin

SIZE
To fit age

| 3-4 | 5-6 | 7-8 | 9-10 | 11-12 | years |

YARN
Rowan Colourscape Chunky

| 4 | 5 | 5 | 6 | 7 | x 100gm |

(photographed in Autumn 438)

NEEDLES
1 pair 12mm (US 17) needles

TENSION
9½ sts and 16 rows to 10 cm measured over g st using 12mm (US 17) needles and yarn DOUBLE.

BACK
Using 12mm (US 17) needles and yarn DOUBLE cast on 35 [37: 39: 41: 43] sts.

Work in g st until back meas 24 [25: 26: 27: 28] cm, ending with RS facing for next row.

Shape armholes
Cast off 2 sts at beg of next 2 rows. 31 [33: 35: 37: 39] sts.

Dec 1 st at each end of next and foll 1 [1: 0: 0: 0] alt row. 27 [29: 33: 35: 37] sts.
Cont straight until armhole meas 14 [15: 16: 17: 18] cm, ending with RS facing for next row.

Shape shoulders and back neck
Cast off 3 [3: 4: 4: 5] sts at beg of next 2 rows, then 4 [4: 5: 5: 5] sts at beg of foll 2 rows.

Cast off rem 13 [15: 15: 17: 17] sts.

FRONT
Work as given for back until 6 rows less have been worked than on back to beg of shoulder shaping, ending with RS facing for next row.

Shape front neck
Next row (RS): K11 [11: 13: 13: 14] and turn, leaving rem sts on a holder.

Work each side of neck separately.

Dec 1 st at neck edge of next 3 rows, then on foll alt row, ending with RS facing for next row. 7 [7: 9: 9: 10] sts.

Shape shoulder
Cast off 3 [3: 4: 4: 5] sts at beg of next row.
Work 1 row.

Cast off rem 4 [4: 5: 5: 5] sts.

With RS facing, rejoin yarn to rem sts, cast off centre 5 [7: 7: 9: 9] sts, K to end.

Complete to match first side, reversing shapings.

SLEEVES
Using 12mm (US 17) needles and yarn DOUBLE cast on 18 [20: 20: 22: 22] sts.

Work in g st, shaping sides by inc 1 st at each end of 13th [15th: 13th: 13th: 11th] and every foll 14th [16th: 14th: 16th: 14th] row to 22 [24: 28: 30: 32] sts, then on every foll 16th [18th: –: –: –] row until there are 24 [26: –: –: –] sts.

Cont straight until sleeve meas 31 [35: 39: 43: 47] cm, ending with RS facing for next row.

Shape top
Cast off 2 sts at beg of next 2 rows. 20 [22: 24: 26: 28] sts.

Dec 1 st at each end of next 6 [3: 3: 3: 3] rows, then on foll 0 [1: 1: 2: 2] alt rows, then on foll 0 [3: 3: 3: 3] rows, ending with RS facing for next row.

Cast off rem 8 [8: 10: 10: 12] sts.

MAKING UP
Press as described on the information page.

Join both shoulder seams using back stitch, or mattress stitch if preferred.

See information page for finishing instructions, setting in sleeves using the set-in method.

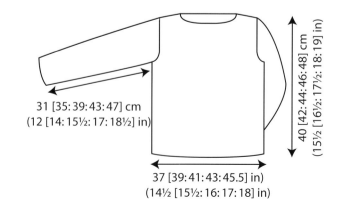

31 [35: 39: 43: 47] cm
(12 [14: 15½: 17: 18½] in)

40 [42: 44: 46: 48] cm
(15½ [16½: 17½: 18: 19] in)

37 [39: 41: 43: 45.5] in)
(14½ [15½: 16: 17: 18] in)

Frances
By Lisa Richardson

Main Image Page 16

YARN
Rowan Felted Tweed

A Bilberry	151	1	x 50gm
B Watery	152	1	x 50gm
C Ginger	154	1	x 50gm
D Gilt	160	1	x 50gm
E Paisley	171	1	x 50gm
F Avocado	161	1	x 50gm

CROCHET HOOK
4mm (no 8) (US G6) crochet hook

TENSION
Basic motif measures 14 cm (5½ ins) square using 4mm (US G6) hook.

FINISHED SIZE
Completed scarf measures 42 cm (16½ ins) wide and 168 cm (66 ins) long.

CROCHET ABBREVIATIONS
ch = chain; **ss** = slip stitch; **dc** = double crochet; **htr** = half treble; **tr** = treble; **sp(s)** = space(s).

BASIC MOTIF
Using 4mm (US G6) hook and first colour make 6 ch and join with a ss to form a ring.

Round 1 (RS): 1 ch (does NOT count as st), 16 dc into ring, ss to first dc. 16 sts.

Round 2: 6 ch (counts as 1 tr and 3 ch), miss first 2 dc, (1 tr into next dc, 3 ch, miss 1 dc) 7 times, ss to 3rd of 6 ch at beg of round. 8 ch sps.

Round 3: 1 ch (does NOT count as st), (1 dc, 1 htr, 5 tr, 1 htr and 1 dc) into each ch sp to end, ss to first dc. 8 petals made.

Fasten off first colour.

Join in 2nd colour between 2 petals and cont as folls:

Round 4: 1 ch (does NOT count as st), 1 dc between 2 petals where yarn was re-joined, ★6 ch, 1 dc between next 2 petals, rep from ★ to end, replacing dc at end of last rep with ss to first dc. 8 ch sps.

Round 5: 1 ch (does NOT count as st), (1 dc, 1 htr, 6 tr, 1 htr and 1 dc) into each ch sp to end, ss to first dc. 8 petals made.

Fasten off 2nd colour.

Join in 3rd colour to 2nd tr (4th st) of one petal and cont as folls:

Round 6: 1 ch (does NOT count as st), 1 dc into tr where yarn was rejoined, ★6 ch, miss 2 tr, 1 dc into next tr★★, 6 ch, 1 dc into 2nd tr (4th st) of next petal, rep from ★ to end, ending last rep at ★★, 3 ch, 1 tr into first dc. 16 ch sps.

Round 7: 3 ch (counts as 1 tr), 3 tr into ch sp partly formed by tr at end of previous round, ★4 ch, 1 dc into next ch sp, (6 ch, 1 dc into next ch sp) twice, 4 ch★★, (4 tr, 4 ch and 4 tr) into next ch sp, rep from ★ to end, ending last rep at ★★, 4 tr into same ch sp as used at beg of round, 4 ch, ss to top of 3 ch at beg of round.

Fasten off.

Basic motif is a square. In each corner there is a 4-ch loop with 4 tr each side. Along each edge there are a further 4 ch sps – two 4-ch loops and two 6-ch loops. Join motifs whilst working round 7 by replacing each (4 ch) with (2 ch, ss into corresponding ch sp along edge of adjacent motif, 2 ch) and each (6 ch) with (3 ch, ss into corresponding ch sp along edge of adjacent motif, 3 ch).

SCARF
Make and join 36 basic motifs to form a rectangle 3 motifs wide and 12 motifs long. Use colours at random but try to distribute colours evenly.

MAKING UP
Press as described on the information page.

Main Image Page 34

Grace ❖ ❖ ❖

By Lisa Richardson

SIZE
To fit age

     3-4   5-6   7-8   years

YARN
Rowan British Sheep Breeds DK

     7   8   8   x 50gm

(photographed in Brown Bluefaced Leicester 781)

NEEDLES
1 pair 3¼mm (no 10) (US 3) needles
1 pair 4mm (no 8) (US 6) needles
2 cable needles

BUTTONS - 7 x BN1367 (15mm) from Bedecked. Please see credits page for contact details.

TENSION
22 sts and 30 rows to 10 cm measured over st st, 33 sts and 34 rows to 10 cm measured over yoke patt, both using 4mm (US 6) needles.

BACK
Using 3¼mm (US 3) needles cast on 98 [104: 108] sts.
Work in g st for 4 rows, ending with RS facing for next row.
Change to 4mm (US 6) needles.
Beg with a K row, work in st st, shaping side seams by dec 1 st at each end of 19th and 5 foll 10th rows. 86 [92: 96] sts.
Work 15 rows, ending with RS facing for next row.
Inc 1 st at each end of next row. 88 [94: 98] sts.
Cont straight until back meas 32 [33: 34] cm, ending with **WS** facing for next row.
Next row (WS): P32 [35: 37], slip next 4 sts onto first cable needle, slip next 4 sts onto 2nd cable needle, fold work so that sts on cable needles are WS facing and RS of sts on 2nd cable needle are against RS of sts on left needle, P tog first st on first cable needle with corresponding st on 2nd cable needle **and** first st on left needle (3 sts), (P tog next 3 sts in same way) 3 times – first half of pleat completed, slip next 4 sts onto first cable needle, slip

next 4 sts onto 2nd cable needle, fold work so that sts on cable needles are RS facing and WS of sts on 2nd cable needle are against WS of sts on left needle, P tog first st on left needle with corresponding st on 2nd cable needle and first st on first cable needle (3 sts), (P tog next 3 sts in same way) 3 times – second half of pleat completed, P32 [35: 37]. 72 [78: 82] sts.
Change to 3¼mm (US 3) needles.
Work in g st for 4 rows, ending with RS facing for next row.
Next row (RS): K1 [0: 0], (K1, M1, K1) 35 [39: 41] times, K1 [0: 0]. 107 [117: 123] sts.
Change to 4mm (US 6) needles.
Now work in yoke patt as folls:
Row 1 (WS): Knit.
Row 2: P1, ★K1 tbl, P1, rep from ★ to end.
These 2 rows form yoke patt.
Cont in patt, inc 1 st at each end of 2nd and 3 [2: 2] foll 4th [6th: 6th] rows, taking inc sts into patt. 115 [123: 129] sts.
Cont straight until back meas 40 [42: 44] cm, ending with RS facing for next row.
Shape armholes
Keeping patt correct, cast off 6 sts at beg of next 2 rows. 103 [111: 117] sts.
Dec 1 st at each end of next 7 [7: 5] rows, then on foll 5 [4: 4] alt rows. 79 [89: 99] sts.
Cont straight until armhole meas 14 [15: 16] cm, ending with RS facing for next row.
Shape shoulders and back neck
Cast off 5 [7: 8] sts at beg of next 2 rows. 69 [75: 83] sts.
Next row (RS): Cast off 5 [7: 8] sts, patt until there are 10 [10: 11] sts on right needle and turn, leaving rem sts on a holder.
Work each side of neck separately.
Cast off 4 sts at beg of next row.
Cast off rem 6 [6: 7] sts.
With RS facing, rejoin yarn to rem sts, cast off centre 39 [41: 45] sts, patt to end.
Complete to match first side, reversing shapings.

LEFT FRONT
Using 3¼mm (US 3) needles cast on 53 [56: 58] sts.

Work in g st for 4 rows, ending with RS facing for next row.
Change to 4mm (US 6) needles.
Beg with a K row, work in st st, shaping side seam by dec 1 st at beg of 19th and 5 foll 10th rows. 47 [50: 52] sts.
Work 15 rows, ending with RS facing for next row.
Inc 1 st at beg of next row. 48 [51: 53] sts.
Cont straight until left front meas 32 [33: 34] cm, ending with **WS** facing for next row.
Next row (WS): P10 [11: 12], slip next 3 sts onto first cable needle, slip next 3 sts onto 2nd cable needle, fold work so that sts on cable needles are WS facing and RS of sts on 2nd cable needle are against RS of sts on left needle, P tog first st on first cable needle with corresponding st on 2nd cable needle **and** first st on left needle (3 sts), (P tog next 3 sts in same way) twice – first half of pleat completed, slip next 3 sts onto first cable needle, slip next 3 sts onto 2nd cable needle, fold work so that sts on cable needles are RS facing and WS of sts on 2nd cable needle are against WS of sts on left needle, P tog first st on left needle with corresponding st on 2nd cable needle and first st on first cable needle (3 sts), (P tog next 3 sts in same way) twice – second half of pleat completed, P20 [22: 23]. 36 [39: 41] sts.
Change to 3¼mm (US 3) needles.
Work in g st for 4 rows, ending with RS facing for next row.
Next row (RS): K1, (K1, M1, K1) 17 [19: 20] times, K1 [0: 0]. 53 [58: 61] sts.
Change to 4mm (US 6) needles.
Now work in yoke patt as folls:
Row 1 (WS): Knit.
Row 2: ★P1, K1 tbl, rep from ★ to last 1 [0: 1] st, P1 [0: 1].
These 2 rows form yoke patt.
Cont in patt, inc 1 st at beg of 2nd and 3 [2: 2] foll 4th [6th: 6th] rows, taking inc sts into patt. 57 [61: 64] sts.
Cont straight until left front matches back to beg of armhole shaping, ending with RS facing for next row.
Shape armhole
Keeping patt correct, cast off 6 sts at beg of next row. 51 [55: 58] sts.
Work 1 row.
Dec 1 st at armhole edge of next 7 [7: 5] rows, then on foll 5 [4: 4] alt rows. 39 [44: 49] sts.
Cont straight until 11 rows less have been worked than on back to beg of shoulder shaping, ending with **WS** facing for next row.
Shape neck
Keeping patt correct, cast off 14 [15: 17] sts at beg of next row. 25 [29: 32] sts.
Dec 1 st at neck edge of next 8 rows, then on foll alt row, ending with RS facing for next row. 16 [20: 23] sts.
Shape shoulder
Cast off 5 [7: 8] sts at beg of next and foll alt row.
Work 1 row.
Cast off rem 6 [6: 7] sts.

RIGHT FRONT
Using 3¼mm (US 3) needles cast on 53 [56: 58] sts.
Work in g st for 4 rows, ending with RS facing for next row.
Change to 4mm (US 6) needles.
Beg with a K row, work in st st, shaping side seam by dec 1 st at end of 19th and 5 foll 10th rows. 47 [50: 52] sts.
Work 15 rows, ending with RS facing for next row.
Inc 1 st at end of next row. 48 [51: 53] sts.
Cont straight until right front meas 32 [33: 34] cm, ending with **WS** facing for next row.
Next row (WS): P20 [22: 23], slip next 3 sts onto first cable needle, slip next 3 sts onto 2nd cable needle, fold work so that sts on cable needles are WS facing and RS of sts on 2nd cable needle are against RS of sts on left needle, P tog first st on first cable needle with corresponding st on 2nd cable needle **and** first st on left needle (3 sts), (P tog next 3 sts in same way) twice – first half of pleat completed, slip next 3 sts onto first cable needle, slip next 3 sts onto 2nd cable needle, fold work so that sts on cable needles are RS facing and WS of sts on 2nd cable needle are against WS of sts on left needle, P tog first st on left needle with corresponding st on 2nd cable needle and first st on first cable needle (3 sts), (P tog next 3 sts in same way) twice – second half of pleat completed, P10 [11: 12]. 36 [39: 41] sts.
Change to 3¼mm (US 3) needles.
Work in g st for 4 rows, ending with RS facing for next row.
Next row (RS): K1 [0: 0], (K1, M1, K1) 17 [19: 20] times, K1. 53 [58: 61] sts.
Change to 4mm (US 6) needles.
Now work in yoke patt as folls:
Row 1 (WS): Knit.
Row 2: P1 [0: 1], ★K1 tbl, P1, rep from ★ to end.
These 2 rows form yoke patt.
Complete to match left front, reversing shapings.

SLEEVES
Using 3¼mm (US 3) needles cast on 40 [42: 44] sts.
Work in g st for 4 rows, ending with RS facing for next row.
Change to 4mm (US 6) needles.
Beg with a K row, work in st st, shaping sides by inc 1 st at each end of 7th [9th: 11th] and every foll 8th [10th: 12th] row to 46 [54: 62] sts, then on every foll 10th [12th: -] row until there are 58 [60: -] sts.
Cont straight until sleeve meas 33 [37: 41] cm, ending with RS facing for next row.
Shape top
Cast off 4 sts at beg of next 2 rows. 50 [52: 54] sts.
Dec 1 st at each end of next 5 rows, then on every foll alt row to 28 sts, then on foll 7 rows, ending with RS facing for next row.
Cast off rem 14 sts.

MAKING UP

Press as described on the information page.

Join both shoulder seams using back stitch, or mattress stitch if preferred.

Button band

With RS facing and using 3¼mm (US 3) needles, pick up and knit 112 [119: 125] sts evenly down entire left front opening edge, from neck shaping to cast-on edge.

Work in g st for 4 rows, ending with **WS** facing for next row.

Cast off knitwise (on **WS**).

Buttonhole band

With RS facing and using 3¼mm (US 3) needles, pick up and knit 112 [119: 125] sts evenly up entire right front opening edge, from cast-on edge to neck shaping.

Row 1 (WS): Knit.

Row 2: K36 [37: 37], *yfwd, K2tog (to make a buttonhole), K10 [11: 12], rep from * 5 times more, yfwd, K2tog (to make 7th buttonhole), K2.

Work in g st for a further 2 rows, ending with **WS** facing for next row.

Cast off knitwise (on **WS**).

Collar

With RS facing and using 3¼mm (US 3) needles, beg and ending halfway across top of bands, pick up and knit 27 [28: 30] sts up right side of neck, 31 [33: 35] sts from back, then 27 [28: 30] sts down left side of neck. 85 [89: 95] sts.

Row 1 (RS of collar, WS of body): K2 [4: 2], inc in next st, (K4, inc in next st) 16 [16: 18] times, K2 [4: 2]. 102 [106: 114] sts.

Row 2: K2, P to last 2 sts, K2.

Row 3: Knit.

Rep last 2 rows until collar meas 6 cm, ending with RS facing for next row.

Work in g st for 3 rows, ending with **WS** facing for next row.

Using a 4mm (US 6) needle, cast off loosely knitwise (on **WS**).

See information page for finishing instructions, setting in sleeves using the set-in method.

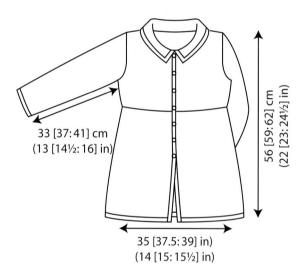

33 [37: 41] cm
(13 [14½: 16] in)

56 [59: 62] cm
(22 [23: 24½] in)

35 [37.5: 39] in)
(14 [15: 15½] in)

Harry
By Lisa Richardson

Main Image Page 4 & 39

SIZE
To fit age

| 3-4 | 5-6 | 7-8 | 9-10 | 11-12 | years |

YARN
Rowan Wool Cotton

	1st colourway			2nd colourway		
A	French Navy 909			Coffee Rich 956		
	3	3	4	4	4	x 50gm
B	Cypress 968			Bronze 967		
	2	2	2	3	3	x 50gm
C	Ship Shape 955			Chestnut 966		
	2	2	2	3	3	x 50gm

NEEDLES
1 pair 3¼mm (no 10) (US 3) needles
1 pair 4mm (no 8) (US 6) needles

TENSION
22 sts and 30 rows to 10 cm measured over st st using 4mm (US 6) needles.

Pattern note: Same chart is used for back and front but appearance of chart is reversed. On back **and** front, work odd numbered rows as K rows and even numbered rows as P rows. On back, work K rows reading chart from right to left and P rows reading chart from left to right. On front, reverse position of design by working K rows reading chart from **left to right** and P rows reading chart from **right to left.**

BACK
Using 3¼mm (US 3) needles and yarn A cast on 77 [80: 86: 92: 95] sts.
Row 1 (RS): P2, ★K1, P2, rep from ★ to end.
Row 2: K2, ★P1, K2, rep from ★ to end.
These 2 rows form rib.
Work in rib for a further 14 rows, - [inc: dec: dec: -] 1 st at end of last row and ending with RS facing for next row. 77 [81: 85: 91: 95] sts.
Change to 4mm (US 6) needles.
Beg and ending rows as indicated, beg with chart row 13 [9: 7: 3: 1] and using the **intarsia** technique as described on the information page, now work in patt from chart, which is worked entirely in st st beg with a K row (see pattern note), as folls:
Work 66 [70: 72: 76: 78] rows, ending after chart row 78 and with RS facing for next row. (Back should meas 27 [28: 29: 30: 31] cm.)
Shape armholes
Keeping patt correct, cast off 3 sts at beg of next 2 rows. 71 [75: 79: 85: 89] sts.
Dec 1 st at each end of next 3 [3: 3: 3: 1] rows, then on foll 4 [3: 1: 1: 2] alt rows. 57 [63: 71: 77: 83] sts.
Cont straight until chart row 118 [120: 124: 126: 130] has been completed, ending with RS facing for next row. (Armhole should meas 13 [14: 15: 16: 17] cm.)
Shape back neck and shoulders
Cast off 4 [5: 6: 7: 8] sts at beg of next 2 rows. 49 [53: 59: 63: 67] sts.
Next row (RS): Cast off 4 [5: 6: 7: 8] sts, K until there are 8 [8: 9: 9: 10] sts on right needle and turn, leaving rem sts on a holder.
Work each side of neck separately.
Cast off 3 sts at beg of next row.
Cast off rem 5 [5: 6: 6: 7] sts.
With RS facing, rejoin appropriate yarns to rem sts, cast off centre 25 [27: 29: 31: 31] sts, K to end.
Complete to match first side, reversing shapings.

FRONT
Reversing position of chart (see pattern note), work as given for back until 10 [10: 10: 12: 12] rows less have been worked than on back to beg of shoulder shaping, ending with RS facing for next row.
Shape front neck
Next row (RS): K18 [20: 23: 26: 29] and turn, leaving rem sts on a holder.
Work each side of neck separately. (**Note:** Front neck shaping is **NOT** shown on chart.)
Dec 1 st at neck edge of next 4 rows, then on foll 1 [1: 1: 2: 2] alt rows. 13 [15: 18: 20: 23] sts.
Work 3 rows, ending with RS facing for next row.
Shape shoulder
Cast off 4 [5: 6: 7: 8] sts at beg of next and foll alt row.
Work 1 row.

Cast off rem 5 [5: 6: 6: 7] sts.

With RS facing, rejoin appropriate yarns to rem sts, cast off centre 21 [23: 25: 25: 25] sts, K to end.

Complete to match first side, reversing shapings.

LEFT SLEEVE STRIPE SEQUENCE

Rows 1 to 14: Using yarn B.

Rows 15 to 28: Using yarn C.

Rows 29 to 42: Using yarn A.

These 42 rows form stripe sequence for **left** sleeve and are repeated.

RIGHT SLEEVE STRIPE SEQUENCE

Rows 1 and 2: Using yarn B.

Rows 3 and 4: Using yarn C.

Rows 5 and 6: Using yarn A.

These 6 rows form stripe sequence for **right** sleeve and are repeated.

SLEEVES

Using 3¼mm (US 3) needles and yarn A cast on 38 [38: 41: 44: 47] sts.

Work in rib as given for back for 16 rows, dec [inc: –: inc: –] 1 st at end of last row and ending with RS facing for next row. 37 [39: 41: 45: 47] sts.

Change to 4mm (US 6) needles.

Joining in colours as required and beg with stripe row 1, now work in st st (beg with a K row) in appropriate stripe sequence (see above), shaping sides by inc 1 st at each end of 3rd [5th: 5th: 7th: 9th] and every foll 6th [6th: 8th: 8th: 10th] row to 61 [53: 65: 49: 61] sts, then on every foll – [8th: –: 10th: 12th] row until there are – [63: –: 67: 69] sts.

Cont straight until sleeve meas 32 [36: 40: 44: 48] cm, ending with RS facing for next row.

Shape top

Keeping stripes correct, cast off 6 [5: 4: 3: 3] sts at beg of next 2 [6: 6: 4: 10] rows, then 7 [6: 5: 4: 4] sts at beg of foll 4 [2: 4: 8: 4] rows.

Cast off rem 21 [21: 21: 23: 23] sts.

MAKING UP

Press as described on the information page.

Join right shoulder seam using back stitch, or mattress stitch if preferred.

Neckband

With RS facing, using 3¼mm (US 3) needles and yarn A, pick up and knit 11 [11: 11: 13: 13] sts down left side of neck, 21 [24: 25: 25: 25] sts from front, 11 [11: 11: 13: 13] sts up right side of neck, then 31 [34: 36: 38: 38] sts from back. 74 [80: 83: 89: 89] sts.

Beg with row 2, work in rib as given for back for 15 rows, ending with RS facing for next row.

Using a 4mm (US 6) needle, cast off **loosely** in rib.

See information page for finishing instructions, setting in sleeves using the shallow set-in method.

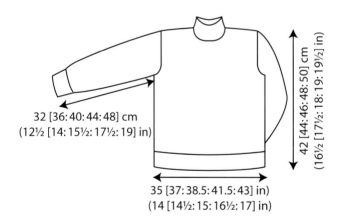

32 [36: 40: 44: 48] cm
(12½ [14: 15½: 17½: 19] in)

42 [44: 46: 48: 50] cm
(16½ [17½: 18: 19: 19½] in)

35 [37: 38.5: 41.5: 43] in)
(14 [14½: 15: 16½: 17] in)

134

130

120

110

100

90

80

70

60

50

40

30

20

10

⌐3-4
⌐5-6
⌐7-8
⌐9-10
⌐11-12

key

A

● B

⊠ C

3-4⌐
5-6⌐
7-8⌐
9-10⌐
11-12⌐

65

Main Image Page 21

Imogen ❖ ❖
By Grace Melville

SIZE
To fit age

| 7–8 | 9–10 | 11–12 | years |

YARN
Rowan Cocoon

A Bilberry 812

| | 3 | 3 | 3 | x 100gm |

B Scree 803

| | 2 | 2 | 3 | x 100gm |

NEEDLES
1 pair 6mm (no 4) (US 10) needles
1 pair 7mm (no 2) (US 10½) needles

TENSION
17 sts and 29 rows to 10 cm measured over patt using 7mm (US 10½) needles.

SPECIAL ABBREVIATIONS
wrap 3 = *slip last 3 sts on right needle back onto left needle keeping yarn at back (WS) of work, bring yarn to front (RS) of work between needles, slip same 3 sts back onto right needle, take yarn back to back (WS) of work, rep from * once more; **up 1** = pick up next dropped (elongated) st and K this st.

Pattern note: When working patt, slip all sts purlwise with yarn at **wrong side** of work – this is **back** of work on RS rows, and **front** of work on WS rows.

BACK
Using 7mm (US 10½) needles and yarn B cast on 73 [81: 89] sts.
Work in g st for 3 rows, ending with **WS** facing for next row.
Row 4 (WS): K1, *K1 wrapping yarn twice round needle, K5, K1 wrapping yarn twice round needle, K1, rep from * to end.
Join in yarn A and now work in patt as folls:
Row 1 (RS): Using yarn A, K1, *sl 1 dropping extra loop, K5, sl 1 dropping extra loop, K1, rep from * to end.
Row 2: Using yarn A, P1, *sl 1, P5, sl 1, P1, rep from * to end.
Row 3: Using yarn A, K1, *sl 1, K5, sl 1, K1, rep from * to end.

Row 4: Using yarn A, P1, *drop next st off needle and leave at back (RS) of work, P5, drop next st off needle and leave at back (RS) of work, P1, rep from * to end.
Row 5: Using yarn B, K1, sl 1, K1, *up 1, K1, up 1, wrap 3, K1, (sl 1) 3 times, K1, rep from * to last 6 sts, up 1, K1, up 1, wrap 3, K1, sl 1, K1.
Row 6: Using yarn B, P1, sl 1, *(P1, P1 wrapping yarn twice round needle) twice, P1, (sl 1) 3 times, rep from * to last 7 sts, (P1, P1 wrapping yarn twice round needle) twice, P1, sl 1, P1.
Row 7: Using yarn A, K3, *sl 1 dropping extra loop, K1, sl 1 dropping extra loop, K5, rep from * to last 6 sts, sl 1 dropping extra loop, K1, sl 1 dropping extra loop, K3.
Row 8: Using yarn A, P3, *sl 1, P1, sl 1, P5, rep from * to last 6 sts, sl 1, P1, sl 1, P3.
Row 9: Using yarn A, K3, *sl 1, K1, sl 1, K5, rep from * to last 6 sts, sl 1, K1, sl 1, K3.
Row 10: Using yarn A, P3, *drop next st off needle and leave at back (RS) of work, P1, drop next st off needle and leave at back (RS) of work, P5, rep from * to last 6 sts, drop next st off needle and leave at back (RS) of work, P1, drop next st off needle and leave at back (RS) of work, P3.
Row 11: Using yarn B, K1, up 1, K1, (sl 1) 3 times, K1, *up 1, K1, up 1, wrap 3, K1, (sl 1) 3 times, K1, rep from * to last st, up 1, K1.
Row 12: Using yarn B, P1, *P1 wrapping yarn twice round needle, P1, (sl 1) 3 times, P1, P1 wrapping yarn twice round needle, P1, rep from * to end.
These 12 rows form patt.
Cont in patt, dec 1 st at each end of 7th and 1 [3: 5] foll 24th [16th: 12th] rows. 69 [73: 77] sts.
Cont straight until back meas 30 cm, ending with RS facing for next row.
Shape for cap sleeves
Inc 1 st at each end of next and foll 1 [1: 3] alt rows, then on foll 0 [2: 2] rows, ending with **WS** facing for next row. 73 [81: 89] sts.
Place markers at both ends of last row to denote base of armhole openings.
Cont straight until armhole meas 15 [16: 17] cm from markers, ending with RS facing for next row.
Shape back neck and shoulders
Next row (RS): Cast off 7 [8: 9] sts, patt until there are 19 [21: 24] sts on right needle and turn, leaving rem sts on a holder.
Work each side of neck separately.

Cast off 3 sts at beg of next row, 7 [8: 9] sts at beg of foll row, then 3 sts at beg of foll row.

Cast off rem 6 [7: 9] sts.

With RS facing, rejoin appropriate yarn to rem sts, cast off centre 21 [23: 23] sts, patt to end.

Complete to match first side, reversing shapings.

FRONT

Work as given for back until 6 rows less have been worked than on back to beg of shoulder shaping, ending with RS facing for next row.

Shape front neck

Next row (RS): Patt 25 [28: 32] sts and turn, leaving rem sts on a holder.

Work each side of neck separately.

Dec 1 st at neck edge of next 5 rows, ending with RS facing for next row. 20 [23: 27] sts.

Shape shoulder

Cast off 7 [8: 9] sts at beg of next and foll alt row.

Work 1 row.

Cast off rem 6 [7: 9] sts.

With RS facing, rejoin appropriate yarn to rem sts, cast off centre 23 [25: 25] sts, patt to end.

Complete to match first side, reversing shapings.

MAKING UP

Press as described on the information page.

Join right shoulder seam using back stitch, or mattress stitch if preferred.

Neckband

With RS facing, using 6mm (US 10) needles and yarn B, pick up and knit 9 sts down left side of neck, 23 [25: 25] sts from front, 9 sts up right side of neck, then 33 [35: 35] sts from back. 74 [78: 78] sts.

Work in g st for 2 rows, ending with **WS** facing for next row.

Cast off knitwise (on **WS**).

Join left shoulder and neckband seam.

Armhole borders (both alike)

With RS facing, using 6mm (US 10) needles and yarn B, pick up and knit 50 [54: 58] sts along armhole edge between markers.

Work in g st for 2 rows, ending with **WS** facing for next row.

Cast off knitwise (on **WS**).

See information page for finishing instructions.

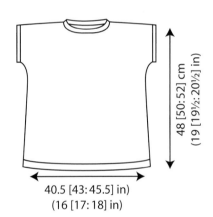

48 [50: 52] cm
(19 [19½: 20½] in)

40.5 [43: 45.5] in)
(16 [17: 18] in)

Main Image Page 18

Jacob ❖ ❖
By Lisa Richardson

SIZE
To fit age

7-8	9-10	11-12	years

YARN
Rowan Felted Tweed Chunky and Colourscape Chunky

A Felted Tweed Chunky
   Blue Shadow 284

6	6	7	x 50gm

B Colourscape Chunky
   Moody Blues 444

2	3	3	x 100gm

NEEDLES
1 pair 7mm (no 2) (US 10½) needles
7mm (no 2) (US 10½) circular needle

FASTENINGS – 6 large (20mm) press studs

TENSION
13 sts and 14 rows to 10 cm measured over patterned st st, 14 sts and 18 rows to 10 cm measured over st st using yarn B, both using 7mm (US 10½) needles.

BACK
Using 7mm (US 10½) needles and yarn A cast on 55 [57: 59] sts.
Row 1 (RS): K2 [0: 0], P3 [0: 1], ★K3, P3, rep from ★ to last 2 [3: 4] sts, K2 [3: 3], P0 [0: 1].
Row 2: P2 [0: 0], K3 [0: 1], ★P3, K3, rep from ★ to last 2 [3: 4] sts, P2 [3: 3], K0 [0: 1].
These 2 rows form rib.
Cont in rib for a further 7 rows, ending with **WS** facing for next row.
Row 10 (WS): Rib 5 [6: 7], work 2 tog, (rib 12, work 2 tog) 3 times, rib 6 [7: 8]. 51 [53: 55] sts.
Beg and ending rows as indicated, using the **fairisle** technique as described on the information page and repeating the 12 row patt rep throughout, now work in patt from chart, which is worked entirely in st st beg with a K row, as folls:
Cont straight until back meas 29 [30: 31] cm, ending with RS facing for next row.
Shape armholes
Place markers at both ends of last row to denote base of armholes.

Keeping patt correct, dec 1 st at each end of next and foll 2 alt rows. 45 [47: 49] sts.
Cont straight until armhole meas 15 [16: 17] cm, ending with RS facing for next row.
Shape shoulders and back neck
Next row (RS): Cast off 6 sts, patt until there are 9 [9: 10] sts on right needle and turn, leaving rem sts on a holder.
Work each side of neck separately.
Cast off 3 sts at beg of next row.
Cast off rem 6 [6: 7] sts.
With RS facing, rejoin appropriate yarns to rem sts, cast off centre 15 [17: 17] sts, patt to end.
Complete to match first side, reversing shapings.

LEFT FRONT
Using 7mm (US 10½) needles and yarn A cast on 27 [28: 29] sts.
Row 1 (RS): K2 [0: 0], P3 [0: 1], ★K3, P3, rep from ★ to last 4 sts, K4.
Row 2: K1, ★P3, K3, rep from ★ to last 2 [3: 4] sts, P2 [3: 3], K0 [0: 1].
These 2 rows form rib.
Cont in rib for a further 7 rows, ending with **WS** facing for next row.
Row 10 (WS): Rib 5 [6: 6], work 2 tog, rib 12, work 2 tog, rib 6 [6: 7]. 25 [26: 27] sts.
Beg and ending rows as indicated, now work in patt from chart as folls:
Cont straight until left front matches back to beg of armhole shaping, ending with RS facing for next row.
Shape armhole
Place marker at end of last row to denote base of armhole.
Keeping patt correct, dec 1 st at beg of next and foll 2 alt rows. 22 [23: 24] sts.
Cont straight until 7 rows less have been worked than on back to beg of shoulder shaping, ending with **WS** facing for next row.
Shape neck
Keeping patt correct, cast off 2 [3: 3] sts at beg of next row, then 2 sts at beg of foll 3 alt rows, ending with RS facing for next row. 14 [14: 15] sts.
Shape shoulder
Cast off 6 sts at beg of next row, then 2 sts at beg of foll row.
Cast off rem 6 [6: 7] sts.

RIGHT FRONT
Using 7mm (US 10½) needles and yarn A cast on 27 [28: 29] sts.
Row 1 (RS): K1, ★K3, P3, rep from ★ to last 2 [3: 4] sts, K2 [3: 3], P0 [0: 1].

Row 2: P2 [0: 0], K3 [0: 1], ★P3, K3, rep from ★ to last 4 sts, P3, K1.
These 2 rows form rib.
Complete to match left front, reversing shapings.

SLEEVES

Using 7mm (US 10½) needles and yarn A cast on 31 [33: 35] sts.
Work in rib as given for back for 10 rows, ending with RS facing for next row.
Break off yarn A and join in yarn B.
Beg with a K row, work in st st, shaping sides by inc 1 st at each end of 17th [19th: 21st] and 2 [1: 1] foll 18th [20th: 22nd] rows, then on – [22nd: 24th] row. 37 [39: 41] sts.
Cont straight until sleeve meas 39 [43: 47] cm, ending with RS facing for next row.

Shape top
Cast off 6 [6: 7] sts at beg of next 2 rows, then 6 [7: 7] sts at beg of foll 2 rows.
Cast off rem 13 sts.

MAKING UP

Press as described on the information page.
Join both shoulder seams using back stitch, or mattress stitch if preferred.

Front band and collar
With RS facing, using 7mm (US 10½) circular needle and yarn A, beg and ending at cast-on edges, pick up and knit 65 [69: 72] sts up right front opening edge to beg of front neck shaping, 16 [17: 17] sts up right side of neck, 23 [25: 25] sts from back, 16 [17: 17] sts down left side of neck to beg of front neck shaping, then 65 [69: 72] sts down left front opening edge. 185 [197: 203] sts.
Row 1 (WS): K1, ★P3, K3, rep from ★ to last 4 sts, P3, K1.
Row 2: K4, ★P3, K3, rep from ★ to last st, K1.
These 2 rows form rib.
Keeping rib correct, cont as folls:
Row 3 (WS): Rib 104 [111: 114], wrap next st (by slipping next st on

left needle onto right needle, taking yarn to opposite side of work between needles and then slipping same st back onto left needle – when working back across wrapped sts, work the wrapped st and the wrapping loop tog as one st) and turn.
Row 4: Rib 23 [25: 25], wrap next st and turn.
Row 5: Rib 27 [29: 29], wrap next st and turn.
Row 6: Rib 31 [33: 33], wrap next st and turn.
Row 7: Rib 35 [37: 37], wrap next st and turn.
Row 8: Rib 39 [41: 41], wrap next st and turn.
Row 9: Rib 43 [45: 45], wrap next st and turn.
Row 10: Rib 47 [49: 49], wrap next st and turn.
Row 11: Rib 51 [53: 53], wrap next st and turn.
Row 12: Rib 55 [57: 57], wrap next st and turn.
Row 13: Rib to end.
Work in rib across all sts for a further 6 rows, ending with RS facing for next row.
Cast off in rib.
See information page for finishing instructions, setting in sleeves using the shallow set-in method. Fasten fronts by attaching press studs to front band sections – place top stud 2.5 cm below beg of front neck shaping, lowest stud 2.5 cm up from cast-on edge, and rem 4 studs evenly spaced between.

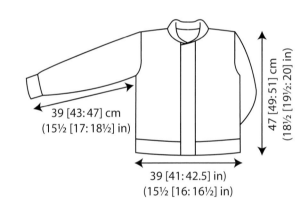

39 [43: 47] cm
(15½ [17: 18½] in)

47 [49: 51] cm
(18½ [19½: 20] in)

39 [41: 42.5] in)
(15½ [16: 16½] in)

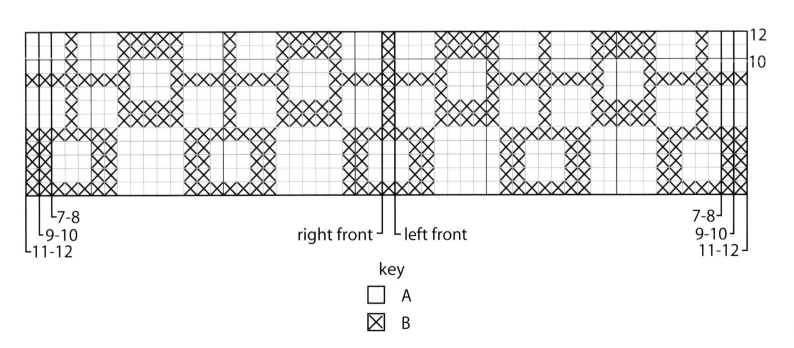

7-8
9-10
11-12

right front | left front

7-8
9-10
11-12

key

☐ A

☒ B

Main Image Page 36

Mabel ❖ ❖
By Marie Wallin

SIZE
To fit age

7-8	9-10	11-12	years

YARN
Rowan Cocoon

4	4	5	x 100gm

(photographed in Lavender Ice 811)

NEEDLES
1 pair 6mm (no 4) (US 10) needles
1 pair 7mm (no 2) (US 10½) needles
Cable needle

TENSION
14 sts and 16 rows to 10 cm measured over st st using 7mm (US 10½) needles.

SPECIAL ABBREVIATIONS
Cr3R = slip next st onto cable needle and leave at back of work, K2, then P1 from cable needle; **Cr3L** = slip next 2 sts onto cable needle and leave at front of work, P1, then K2 from cable needle; **C4B** = slip next 2 sts onto cable needle and leave at back of work, K2, then K2 from cable needle; **C4F** = slip next 2 sts onto cable needle and leave at front of work, K2, then K2 from cable needle; **C6B** = slip next 3 sts onto cable needle and leave at back of work, K3, then K3 from cable needle; **C6F** = slip next 3 sts onto cable needle and leave at front of work, K3, then K3 from cable needle.

BACK
Using 6mm (US 10) needles cast on 90 [90: 92] sts.
Work in g st for 3 rows, ending with **WS** facing for next row.
Row 4 (WS): K0 [0: 1], ★K1, M1, K3, M1, K4, M1, K3, M1, K11, M1, K2, M1, K3, M1, K2, M1, K10, rep from ★ once more, K1, M1, K3, M1, K4, M1, K3, M1, K1 [1: 2]. 110 [110: 112] sts.
Change to 7mm (US 10 1/2) needles.
Now work in patt as folls:
Row 1 (RS): P0 [0: 1], ★work next 16 sts as row 1 of panel A, K9, work next 13 sts as row 1 of panel B, K9, rep from ★ once more, work next 16 sts as row 1 of panel A, P0 [0: 1].
Row 2: K0 [0: 1], ★work next 16 sts as row 2 of panel A, P9, work next 13 sts as row 2 of panel B, P9, rep from ★ once more, work next 16 sts

as row 2 of panel A, K0 [0: 1].
These 2 rows set the sts – 5 panels each with 9 sts in st st between them and 0 [0: 1] st in rev st st at side seam edges.
Keeping sts correct as now set and repeating the 10 and 8 row patt reps throughout, cont as folls:
Work 8 rows, ending with RS facing for next row.
Next row (RS): P0 [0: 1], (patt 16 sts, sl 1, K1, psso, K5, K2tog, patt 13 sts, sl 1, K1, psso, K5, K2tog) twice, patt 16 sts, P0 [0: 1]. 102 [102: 104] sts.
Now working 7 sts in st st between panels (instead of 9 sts), work 7 rows.
Next row (RS): P0 [0: 1], (patt 16 sts, sl 1, K1, psso, K3, K2tog, patt 13 sts, sl 1, K1, psso, K3, K2tog) twice, patt 16 sts, P0 [0: 1]. 94 [94: 96] sts.
Now working 5 sts in st st between panels (instead of 7 sts), work 7 rows.
Next row (RS): P0 [0: 1], (patt 16 sts, sl 1, K1, psso, K1, K2tog, patt 13 sts, sl 1, K1, psso, K1, K2tog) twice, patt 16 sts, P0 [0: 1]. 86 [86: 88] sts.
Now working 3 sts in st st between panels (instead of 5 sts), work 7 rows.
Next row (RS): P0 [0: 1], (patt 16 sts, sl 1, K2tog, psso, patt 13 sts, sl 1, K2tog, psso) twice, patt 16 sts, P0 [0: 1]. 78 [78: 80] sts.
Now working 1 st in st st between panels (instead of 3 sts), cont as folls:
Cont straight until back meas 22 [24: 25] cm, ending with RS facing for next row.

Age 7-8 only
Next row (RS): Patt 14 sts, P2tog, K1, patt 13 sts, K1, P2tog, patt 12 sts, P2tog, K1, patt 13 sts, K1, P2tog, patt 14 sts. 74 sts.
Work 1 row.

All sizes
Change to 6mm (US 10) needles.
Next row (RS): K0 [0: 1], ★K1, K2tog, (K2, K2tog) 3 times, K2 [3: 3], (K2tog, K1) 4 times, K0 [1: 1], rep from ★ once more, K1, K2tog, (K2, K2tog) 3 times, K1 [1: 2]. 54 [58: 60] sts.
Now work in double moss st as folls:
Row 1 (WS): K0 [0: 1], P2, ★K2, P2, rep from ★ to last 0 [0: 1] st, K0 [0: 1].
Rows 2 and 3: P0 [0: 1], K2, ★P2, K2, rep from ★ to last 0 [0: 1] st, P0 [0: 1].
Row 4: As row 1.
These 4 rows form double moss st.
Work in double moss st for a further 4 rows, ending with **WS** facing for next row.
Change to 7mm (US 10½) needles.
Place markers at both ends of last row to denote base of armhole openings.
Beg with a P row, work in st st until work meas 14 [15: 16] cm from

markers, ending with RS facing for next row.

Shape shoulders and back neck

Cast off 3 [3: 4] sts at beg of next 4 rows. 42 [46: 44] sts.

Next row (RS): Cast off 3 [4: 4] sts, K until there are 7 [7: 6] sts on right needle and turn, leaving rem sts on a holder.

Work each side of neck separately.

Cast off 3 sts at beg of next row.

Cast off rem 4 [4: 3] sts.

With RS facing, rejoin yarn to rem sts, cast off centre 22 [24: 24] sts, K to end.

Complete to match first side, reversing shapings.

FRONT

Work as given for back to beg of shoulder shaping, ending with RS facing for next row.

Shape shoulders and front neck

Next row (RS): Cast off 3 [3: 4] sts, K until there are 14 [15: 15] sts on right needle and turn, leaving rem sts on a holder.

Work each side of neck separately.

Dec 1 st at neck edge of next 4 rows **and at same time** cast off 3 [3: 4] sts at beg of 2nd row and 3 [4: 4] sts at beg of foll alt row.

Work 1 row.

Cast off rem 4 [4: 3] sts.

With RS facing, rejoin yarn to rem sts, cast off centre 20 [22: 22] sts, K to end.

Complete to match first side, reversing shapings.

MAKING UP

Press as described on the information page.

Join right shoulder seam using back stitch, or mattress stitch if preferred.

Neckband

With RS facing and using 6mm (US 10) needles, pick up and knit 6 sts down left side of neck, 20 [22: 22] sts from front, 6 sts up right side of neck, then 28 [30: 30] sts from back. 60 [64: 64] sts.

Work in g st for 3 rows, ending with RS facing for next row.

Cast off.

Join left shoulder and neckband seam.

Armhole borders (both alike)

With RS facing and using 6mm (US 10) needles, pick up and knit 40 [42: 44] sts evenly along armhole opening edge between markers.

Row 1 (WS): K1 [0: 1], P2, *K2, P2, rep from * to last 1 [0: 1] st, K1 [0: 1].

Rows 2 and 3: P1 [0: 1], K2, *P2, K2, rep from * to last 1 [0: 1] st, P1 [0: 1].

Row 4: As row 1.

These 4 rows form double moss st.

Work in double moss st for a further 3 rows, ending with RS facing for next row.

Cast off in patt.

See information page for finishing instructions.

Panel A

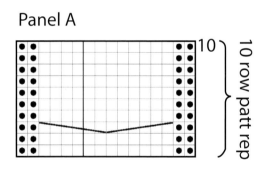

10

10 row patt rep

Panel B

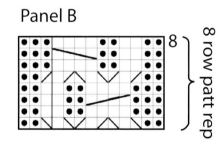

8

8 row patt rep

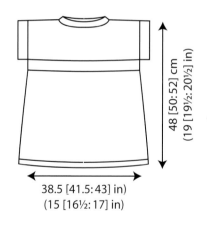

48 [50: 52] cm
(19 [19½: 20½] in)

38.5 [41.5: 43] in)
(15 [16½: 17] in)

key

☐	K on RS, P on WS
⬛	P on RS, K on WS
⟋ ⟍	Cr3R
⟍ ⟍	Cr3L
C4B	C4B
C4F	C4F
C6B	C6B
C6F	C6F

Main Image Page 2

SIZE
To fit age

	3-4	5-6	7-8	9-10	11-12	years

YARN
Rowan Felted Tweed

A Clay 177

	2	2	2	3	3	x 50gm

B Ginger 154

	2	2	2	2	2	x 50gm

C Gilt 160

	2	2	2	2	2	x 50gm

NEEDLES
1 pair 3¼mm (no 10) (US 3) needles
1 pair 4mm (no 8) (US 6) needles

TENSION
24 sts and 43 rows to 10 cm measured over patt using 4mm (US 6) needles.

SPECIAL ABBREVIATION
wyab = with yarn at back (RS) of work.

Pattern note: When working patt, slip all sts purlwise.

BACK
Using 3¼mm (US 3) needles and yarn A cast on 87 [91: 99: 103: 111] sts.
Work in g st for 7 rows, ending with **WS** facing for next row.
Change to 4mm (US 6) needles.
Joining in colours as required, now work in patt as folls:
Row 1 (WS): Using yarn A, P1, sl 1 wyab, *P3, sl 1 wyab, rep from * to last st, P1.
Row 2: Using yarn A, K1, sl 1, *K3, sl 1, rep from * to last st, K1.
Row 3: Using yarn B, P3, *sl 1 wyab, P3, rep from * to end.
Row 4: Using yarn B, K3, *sl 1, K3, rep from * to end.
Row 5: Using yarn C, P1, sl 1 wyab, *P3, sl 1 wyab, rep from * to last st, P1.
Row 6: Using yarn C, K1, sl 1, *K3, sl 1, rep from * to last st, K1.
Row 7: Using yarn A, P3, *sl 1 wyab, P3, rep from * to end.

Row 8: Using yarn A, K3, *sl 1, K3, rep from * to end.
Row 9: Using yarn B, P1, sl 1 wyab, *P3, sl 1 wyab, rep from * to last st, P1.
Row 10: Using yarn B, K1, sl 1, *K3, sl 1, rep from * to last st, K1.
Row 11: Using yarn C, P3, *sl 1 wyab, P3, rep from * to end.
Row 12: Using yarn C, K3, *sl 1, K3, rep from * to end.
These 12 rows form patt.
Cont in patt until back meas 28 [29: 30: 31: 32] cm, ending with RS facing for next row.

Shape armholes
Keeping patt correct, cast off 4 sts at beg of next 2 rows. 79 [83: 91: 95: 103] sts.
Dec 1 st at each end of next 7 [5: 5: 5: 5] rows, then on foll 4 [4: 4: 3: 3] alt rows. 57 [65: 73: 79: 87] sts.
Cont straight until armhole meas 14 [15: 16: 17: 18] cm, ending with RS facing for next row.

Shape back neck and shoulders
Next row (RS): Cast off 2 [3: 4: 4: 5] sts, patt until there are 11 [13: 15: 17: 20] sts on right needle and turn, leaving rem sts on a holder.
Work each side of neck separately.
Dec 1 st at neck edge of next 4 rows **and at same time** cast off 2 [3: 4: 4: 5] sts at beg of 2nd and foll alt row.
Work 1 row.
Cast off rem 3 [3: 3: 5: 6] sts.
With RS facing, rejoin appropriate yarn to rem sts, cast off centre 31 [33: 35: 37: 37] sts, patt to end.
Complete to match first side, reversing shapings.

FRONT
Work as given for back until 18 [18: 18: 22: 22] rows less have been worked than on back to beg of shoulder shaping, ending with RS facing for next row.

Shape front neck
Next row (RS): Patt 19 [22: 25: 28: 32] sts and turn, leaving rem sts on a holder.
Work each side of neck separately.
Dec 1 st at neck edge of next 6 rows, then on foll 3 alt rows, then on 1 [1: 1: 2: 2] foll 4th rows. 9 [12: 15: 17: 21] sts.
Work 1 row, ending with RS facing for next row.

Shape shoulder
Cast off 2 [3: 4: 4: 5] sts at beg of next and foll 2 alt rows.

Work 1 row.

Cast off rem 3 [3: 3: 5: 6] sts.

With RS facing, rejoin appropriate yarn to rem sts, cast off centre 19 [21: 23: 23: 23] sts, patt to end.

Complete to match first side, reversing shapings.

SLEEVES

Using 3¼mm (US 3) needles and yarn A cast on 41 [43: 45: 49: 51] sts.

Work in g st for 6 rows, ending with RS facing for next row.

Row 7 (RS): K0 [0: 0: 2: 1], (K2 [2: 2: 2: 3], M1, K4 [3: 5: 5: 6], M1, K2 [2: 2: 2: 3]) 5 [6: 5: 5: 4] times, K1 [1: 0: 2: 2]. 51 [55: 55: 59: 59] sts.

Change to 4mm (US 6) needles.

Joining in colours as required, now work in patt as given for back, shaping sides by inc 1 st at each end of 14th [20th: 20th: 22nd: 22nd] and every foll 16th [20th: 20th: 22nd: 22nd] row to 65 [61: 65: 65: 73] sts, then on every foll - [22nd: 22nd: 24th: 24th] row until there are - [67: 69: 73: 75] sts, taking inc sts into patt.

Cont straight until sleeve meas 31 [35: 39: 43: 47] cm, ending with RS facing for next row.

Shape top

Keeping patt correct, cast off 4 sts at beg of next 2 rows. 57 [59: 61: 65: 67] sts.

Dec 1 st at each end of next 5 rows, then on every foll alt row until 43 sts rem, then on foll 5 rows, ending with RS facing for next row. 33 sts.

Cast off 4 sts at beg of next 4 rows.

Cast off rem 17 sts.

MAKING UP

Press as described on the information page.

Join right shoulder seam using back stitch, or mattress stitch if preferred.

Neckband

With RS facing, using 3¼mm (US 3) needles and yarn A, pick up and knit 19 [19: 19: 21: 21] sts down left side of neck, 19 [21: 23: 23: 23] sts from front, 19 [19: 19: 21: 21] sts up right side of neck, then 39 [41: 43: 45: 45] sts from back. 96 [100: 104: 110: 110] sts.

Work in g st for 2 rows, ending with **WS** facing for next row.

Cast off knitwise (on **WS**).

See information page for finishing instructions, setting in sleeves using the set-in method.

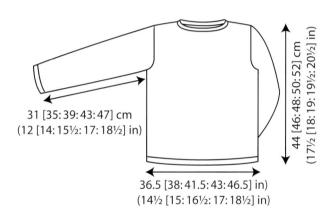

31 [35: 39: 43: 47] cm
(12 [14: 15½: 17: 18½] in)

44 [46: 48: 50: 52] cm
(17½ [18: 19: 19½: 20½] in)

36.5 [38: 41.5: 43: 46.5] in)
(14½ [15: 16½: 17: 18½] in)

Main Image Page 7

Olivia ❖ ❖ ❖
By Marie Wallin

SIZE
To fit age

5-6	7-8	9-10	11-12	years

YARN
Rowan Felted Tweed

	5-6	7-8	9-10	11-12	
A Melody 142	3	4	4	4	x 50gm
B Paisley 171	1	1	1	1	x 50gm
C Duck Egg 173	1	1	1	1	x 50gm
D Grey Mist 164	1	2	2	2	x 50gm
E Avocado 161	1	1	1	1	x 50gm
F Gilt 160	1	1	1	1	x 50gm
G Scree 165	1	1	1	1	x 50gm

NEEDLES
1 pair 3¼mm (no 10) (US 3) needles
2 double-pointed 2¾mm (no 12) (US 2) needles

BUTTONS - 5 x RW5013 (13mm) from Bedecked. Please see credits page for contact details.

TENSION
26 sts and 29 rows to 10 cm measured over patterned st st using 3¼mm (US 3) needles.

BACK
Using 3¼mm (US 3) needles and yarn A cast on 93 [99: 105: 109] sts.
Row 1 (RS): K1, *P1, K1, rep from * to end.
Row 2: As row 1.
These 2 rows form moss st.
Cont in moss st until back meas 12 cm, ending with RS facing for next row.
Next row (eyelet row) (RS): Moss st 4 [3: 2: 4] sts, (yrn, work 2 tog, moss st 2 sts) 10 [11: 12: 12] times, yrn, work 2 tog, moss st 1 st, work 2 tog tbl, yrn, (moss st 2 sts, work 2 tog tbl, yrn) 10 [11: 12: 12] times, moss st 4 [3: 2: 4] sts.
Work in moss st for a further 2 rows, ending with **WS** facing for next row.
Next row (WS): Purl.
Beg and ending rows as indicated and using the **fairisle** technique as described on the information page, now work in patt from chart for body, which is worked entirely in st st beg with a K row, as folls:
Work 38 [40: 44: 46] rows, ending with RS facing for next row. (Back should meas 26 [27: 28: 29] cm.)
Shape armholes
Keeping patt correct, cast off 3 sts at beg of next 2 rows. 87 [93: 99: 103] sts.
Dec 1 st at each end of next 5 [3: 3: 3] rows, then on foll 3 [3: 4: 2] alt rows. 71 [81: 85: 93] sts.
Cont straight until chart row 76 [82: 88: 94] has been completed, ending with RS facing for next row.
Next row (eyelet row) (RS): Patt 17 [22: 20: 24] sts, (yfwd, K2tog, patt 2 sts) 4 [4: 5: 5] times, yfwd, K2tog, patt 1 st, K2tog tbl, yfwd, (patt 2 sts, K2tog tbl, yfwd) 4 [4: 5: 5] times, patt 17 [22: 20: 24] sts.
(**Note:** Eyelet holes are **NOT** shown on chart.)
Work 1 row, ending with RS facing for next row.
Shape shoulders and back neck
Next row (RS): Cast off 5 [7: 7: 8] sts, patt until there are 8 [11: 10: 13] sts on right needle, yfwd, K2tog, patt 41 [41: 47: 47] sts, K2tog tbl, yfwd, patt to end.
Cast off 5 [7: 7: 8] sts at beg of next row. 61 [67: 71: 77] sts.
Next row (RS): Cast off 5 [7: 7: 8] sts, patt until there are 9 [9: 9: 11] sts on right needle and turn, leaving rem sts on a holder.
Work each side of neck separately.
Cast off 3 sts at beg of next row.
Cast off rem 6 [6: 6: 8] sts.
With RS facing, rejoin appropriate yarns to rem sts, cast off centre 33 [35: 39: 39] sts, patt to end.
Complete to match first side, reversing shapings.

LEFT FRONT
Using 3¼mm (US 3) needles and yarn A cast on 47 [50: 53: 55] sts.
Row 1 (RS): *K1, P1, rep from * to last 1 [0: 1: 1] st, K1 [0: 1: 1].
Row 2: K1 [0: 1: 1], *P1, K1, rep from * to end.

These 2 rows form moss st.

Cont in moss st until left front meas 12 cm, ending with RS facing for next row.

Next row (eyelet row) (RS): Moss st 4 [3: 2: 4] sts, yrn, work 2 tog, (moss st 2 sts, yrn, work 2 tog) 10 [11: 12: 12] times, moss st 1 st.

Work in moss st for a further 2 rows, ending with **WS** facing for next row.

Next row (WS): Purl.

Beg and ending rows as indicated, now work in patt from chart for body as folls:

Work 38 [40: 44: 46] rows, ending with RS facing for next row.

Shape armhole

Keeping patt correct, cast off 3 sts at beg of next row. 44 [47: 50: 52] sts.

Work 1 row.

Dec 1 st at armhole edge of next 5 [3: 3: 3] rows, then on foll 3 [3: 4: 2] alt rows. 36 [41: 43: 47] sts.

Cont straight until chart row 66 [72: 76: 82] has been completed, ending with RS facing for next row.

Next row (eyelet row) (RS): Patt 21 [26: 24: 28] sts, (yfwd, K2tog, patt 2 sts) 3 [3: 4: 4] times, yfwd, K2tog, patt 1 st.

(**Note**: Eyelet holes and front neck shaping are **NOT** shown on chart.)

Work 1 row.

Next row: Patt 18 [22: 21: 25] sts, yfwd, K2tog, patt 16 [17: 20: 20] sts.

Work 1 row, ending with RS facing for next row.

Shape neck

Next row (RS): Patt 15 [19: 26: 30] sts, (yfwd, K2tog) 1 [1: 0: 0] times, patt to end.

Break off yarns and slip last 15 [16: 17: 17] sts of this row onto a holder. Rejoin yarns to rem 21 [25: 26: 30] sts with **WS** facing and cont as folls:

Dec 1 st at neck edge of next 3 [3: 1: 1] rows. 18 [22: 25: 29] sts.

Next row: Patt to last 5 [5: 7: 7] sts, yfwd, K2tog, patt 1 [1: 3: 3] sts, K2tog. 17 [21: 24: 28] sts.

9-10 and 11-12 years only

Dec 1 st at neck edge of next 2 rows. – [-: 22: 26] sts.

Work 1 row.

Next row: Patt to last 6 sts, yfwd, K2tog, patt 2 sts, K2tog. – [-: 21: 25] sts.

All sizes

Work 3 rows, dec 1 st at neck edge of 2nd of these rows and ending with RS facing for next row. 16 [20: 20: 24] sts.

Shape shoulder

Next row (RS): Cast off 5 [7: 7: 8] sts, patt until there are 7 [9: 9: 12] sts on right needle, yfwd, K2tog, patt 2 sts.

Work 1 row.

Cast off 5 [7: 7: 8] sts at beg of next row.

Work 1 row.

Cast off rem 6 [6: 6: 8] sts.

RIGHT FRONT

Using 3¼mm (US 3) needles and yarn A cast on 47 [50: 53: 55] sts.

Row 1 (RS): K1 [0: 1: 1], ★P1, K1, rep from ★ to end.

Row 2: ★K1, P1, rep from ★ to last 1 [0: 1: 1] st, K1 [0: 1: 1].

These 2 rows form moss st.

Cont in moss st until back meas 12 cm, ending with RS facing for next row.

Next row (eyelet row) (RS): Moss st 1 st, work 2 tog tbl, yrn, (moss st 2 sts, work 2 tog tbl, yrn) 10 [11: 12: 12] times, moss st 4 [3: 2: 4] sts.

Work in moss st for a further 2 rows, ending with **WS** facing for next row.

Next row (WS): Purl.

Beg and ending rows as indicated, now work in patt from chart for body as folls:

Work 39 [41: 45: 47] rows, ending with **WS** facing for next row.

Shape armhole

Keeping patt correct, cast off 3 sts at beg of next row. 44 [47: 50: 52] sts.

Dec 1 st at armhole edge of next 5 [3: 3: 3] rows, then on foll 3 [3: 4: 2] alt rows. 36 [41: 43: 47] sts.

Cont straight until chart row 66 [72: 76: 82] has been completed, ending with RS facing for next row.

Next row (eyelet row) (RS): Patt 1 st, K2tog tbl, yfwd, (patt 2 sts, K2tog tbl, yfwd) 3 [3: 4: 4] times, patt 21 [26: 24: 28] sts.

(**Note**: Eyelet holes and front neck shaping are **NOT** shown on chart.)

Work 1 row.

Next row: Patt 16 [17: 20: 20] sts, K2tog tbl, yfwd, patt 18 [22: 21: 25] sts.

Work 1 row, ending with RS facing for next row.

Shape neck

Next row (RS): Patt 15 [16: 17: 17] sts and slip these sts onto a holder, (patt 4 sts, K2tog tbl, yfwd) 1 [1: 0: 0] times, patt 15 [19: 26: 30] sts. 21 [25: 26: 30] sts.

Dec 1 st at neck edge of next 3 [3: 1: 1] rows. 18 [22: 25: 29] sts.

Next row: K2tog, patt 1 [1: 3: 3] sts, K2tog tbl, yfwd, patt to end. 17 [21: 24: 28] sts.

9-10 and 11-12 years only

Dec 1 st at neck edge of next 2 rows. – [-: 22: 26] sts.

Work 1 row.

Next row: K2tog, patt 2 sts, K2tog tbl, yfwd, patt to end. – [-: 21: 25] sts.

All sizes

Work 3 rows, dec 1 st at neck edge of 2nd of these rows and ending with RS facing for next row. 16 [20: 20: 24] sts.

Next row (RS): Patt 2 sts, K2tog tbl, yfwd, patt to end.

Shape shoulder

Cast off 5 [7: 7: 8] sts at beg of next and foll alt row.

Work 1 row.

Cast off rem 6 [6: 6: 8] sts.

SLEEVES

Using 3¼mm (US 3) needles and yarn A cast on 63 [65: 67: 69] sts.

Cont in moss st as given for back for 9 cm, ending with RS facing for next row.

Next row (eyelet row) (RS): Moss st 1 [2: 3: 4] sts, (yrn, work 2 tog, moss st 2 sts) 7 times, yrn, work 2 tog, moss st 1 st, work 2 tog tbl, yrn, (moss st 2 sts, work 2 tog tbl, yrn) 7 times, moss st 1 [2: 3: 4] sts.

Work in moss st for a further 2 rows, ending with **WS** facing for next row.

Next row (WS): Purl.

Beg and ending rows as indicated, using the **fairisle** technique as described on the information page and beg with chart row 27 [17: 11: 1], now work in patt from chart for sleeve, which is worked entirely in st st beg with a K row, as folls:

Inc 1 st at each end of 13th [15th: 15th: 17th] and 2 [1: 5: 5] foll 12th [14th: 14th: 16th] rows, then on 3 [4: -: -] foll 10th [12th: -: -] rows, taking inc sts into patt. 75 [77: 79: 81] sts.

Work 9 [11: 13: 13] rows, ending after chart row 102 [104: 108: 110] and with RS facing for next row.

(Sleeve should meas 36 [40: 44: 48] cm.)

Shape top

Keeping patt correct, cast off 3 sts at beg of next 2 rows. 69 [71: 73: 75] sts.

Dec 1 st at each end of next 5 rows, then on every foll alt row to 51 sts, then on foll 9 rows, ending with RS facing for next row. 33 sts.

Cast off 4 sts at beg of next 4 rows.

Cast off rem 17 sts.

MAKING UP

Press as described on the information page.

Join both shoulder seams using back stitch, or mattress stitch if preferred.

Neckband

With RS facing, using 3¼mm (US 3) needles and yarn A, beg and ending at front opening edges, K across 15 [16: 17: 17] sts on right front holder, pick up and knit 9 [9: 11: 11] sts up right side of neck, 39 [41: 45: 45] sts from back, and 9 [9: 11: 11] sts down left side of neck, then K across 15 [16: 17: 17] sts on left front holder. 87 [91: 101: 101] sts.

Work in moss st as given for back for 5 rows, ending with RS facing for next row.

Cast off in moss st.

Button band

With RS facing, using 3¼mm (US 3) needles and yarn A, beg at top of neckband, pick up and knit 67 [71: 75: 79] sts down left front opening edge to top of moss st section.

Work in moss st as given for back for 5 rows, ending with RS facing for next row.

Cast off in moss st.

Buttonhole band

With RS facing, using 3¼mm (US 3) needles and yarn A, beg at top of moss st section, pick up and knit 67 [71: 75: 79] sts up right front opening edge to top of neckband.

Work in moss st as given for back for 1 row, ending with RS facing for next row.

Row 2 (RS): Moss st 3 sts, ★yrn, work 2 tog (to make a buttonhole), moss st 13 [14: 15: 16] sts, rep from ★ 3 times more, yrn, work 2 tog (to make 5th buttonhole), moss st 2 sts.

Work in moss st for a further 3 rows, ending with RS facing for next row.

Cast off in moss st.

See information page for finishing instructions, setting in sleeves using the set-in method.

Waist tie

Using double-pointed 2¾mm (US 2) needles and yarn A cast on 4 sts.

Row 1 (RS): K4, ★without turning slip these 4 sts to opposite end of needle and bring yarn to opposite end of work pulling it quite tightly across **WS** of work, K these 4 sts again, rep from ★ until tie is 105 [110: 110: 115] cm long.

Cast off.

Thread tie through eyelet row at top of moss st section. Make two 3 cm diameter pompons and attach one to each end of tie.

Neck tie

Work as given for waist tie until this tie is 65 [65: 70: 70] cm long.

Cast off.

Thread tie through eyelets around neck edge. Make two 3 cm diameter pompons and attach one to each end of tie.

Sleeve ties (both alike)

Work as given for waist tie until this tie is 55 [55: 60: 60] cm long.

Cast off.

Thread tie through eyelet row at top of moss st section. Make four 3 cm diameter pompons and attach one to each end of each tie.

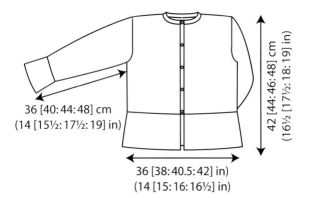

36 [40: 44: 48] cm
(14 [15½: 17½: 19] in)

42 [44: 46: 48] cm
(16½ [17½: 18: 19] in)

36 [38: 40.5: 42] in)
(14 [15: 16: 16½] in)

Body Chart

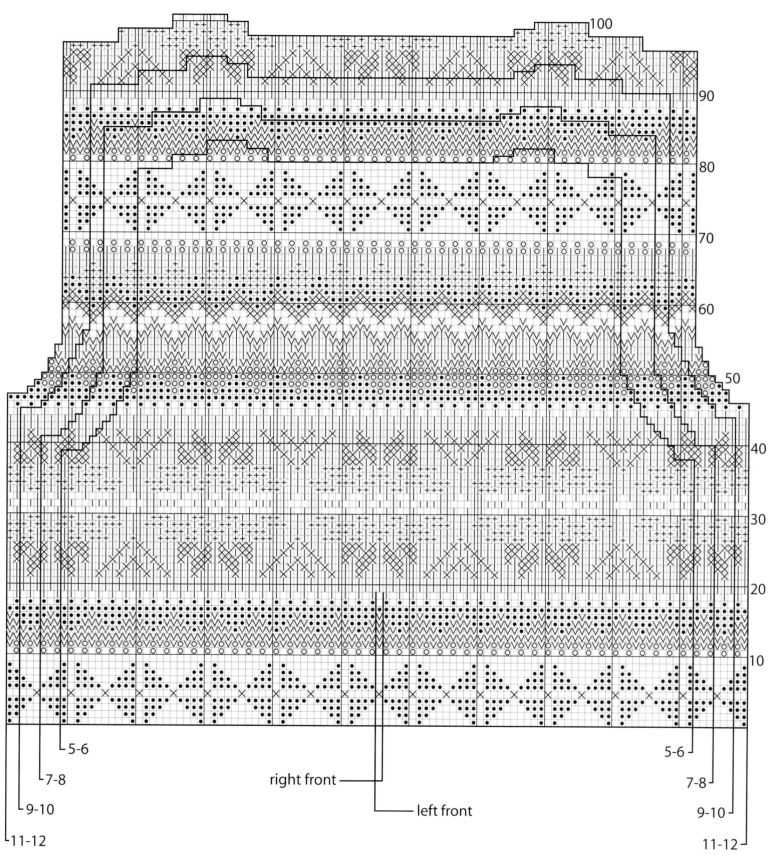

100

90

80

70

60

50

40

30

20

10

5-6

7-8

right front

left front

5-6

7-8

9-10

9-10

11-12

11-12

Sleeve Chart

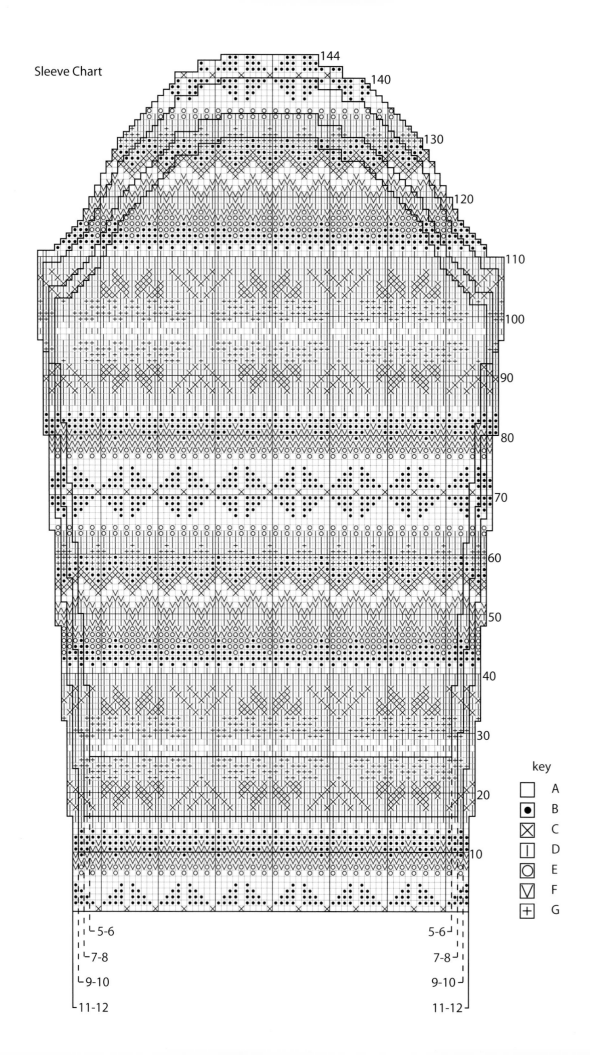

key

☐	A
⬤	B
☒	C
⊡	D
⊙	E
⋁	F
⊞	G

144

140

130

120

110

100

90

80

70

60

50

40

30

20

10

5-6

7-8

9-10

11-12

5-6

7-8

9-10

11-12

Reggie
By Marie Wallin

Main Image Page 30

SIZE
To fit age

| 3-4 | 5-6 | 7-8 | 9-10 | 11-12 | years |

YARN
Rowan Cocoon

| 4 | 5 | 6 | 6 | 7 | x 100gm |

(photographed in Misty Blue 827)

NEEDLES
1 pair 6mm (no 4) (US 10) needles
1 pair 7mm (no 2) (US 10½) needles
6mm (no 4) (US 10) circular needle
Cable needle

BUTTONS – 1 x RW5030 (20mm) from Bedecked. Please see credits page for contact details.

TENSION
18 sts and 19 rows to 10 cm measured over body patt, 17 sts and 19 rows to 10 cm measured over sleeve patt, both using 7mm (US 10½) needles.

SPECIAL ABBREVIATIONS
C4B = slip next 2 sts onto cable needle and leave at back of work, K2, then K2 from cable needle; **C4F** = slip next 2 sts onto cable needle and leave at front of work, K2, then K2 from cable needle.

BACK
Using 6mm (US 10) needles cast on 65 [67: 71: 75: 79] sts.
Row 1 (RS): P0 [1: 0: 0: 1], K2 [2: 1: 1: 2], (P2, K2) 2 [2: 3: 2: 2] times, P3, (K3, P3) 7 [7: 7: 9: 9] times, (K2, P2) 2 [2: 3: 2: 2] times, K2 [2: 1: 1: 2], P0 [1: 0: 0: 1].
Row 2: K0 [1: 0: 0: 1], P2 [2: 1: 1: 2], (K2, P2) 2 [2: 3: 2: 2] times, K3, (P3, K3) 7 [7: 7: 9: 9] times, (P2, K2) 2 [2: 3: 2: 2] times, P2 [2: 1: 1: 2], K0 [1: 0: 0: 1].
These 2 rows form rib.
Work in rib for a further 10 rows, dec 1 st at centre of last row and ending with RS facing for next row. 64 [66: 70: 74: 78] sts.
Change to 7mm (US 10½) needles.
Now work in patt as folls:
Row 1 (RS): K0 [0: 1: 1: 0], P0 [1: 2: 2: 1], (K2, P2) 2 [2: 2: 1: 2] times,

K48 [48: 48: 60: 60], (P2, K2) 2 [2: 2: 1: 2] times, P0 [1: 2: 2: 1], K0 [0: 1: 1: 0].
Row 2 and every foll alt row: P0 [0: 1: 1: 0], K0 [1: 2: 2: 1], (P2, K2) 2 [2: 2: 1: 2] times, P48 [48: 48: 60: 60], (K2, P2) 2 [2: 2: 1: 2] times, K0 [1: 2: 2: 1], P0 [0: 1: 1: 0].
Row 3: K0 [0: 1: 1: 0], P0 [1: 2: 2: 1], (K2, P2) 2 [2: 2: 1: 2] times, (K2, C4F, C4B, K2) 4 [4: 4: 5: 5] times, (P2, K2) 2 [2: 2: 1: 2] times, P0 [1: 2: 2: 1], K0 [0: 1: 1: 0].
Row 5: As row 1.
Row 7: K0 [0: 1: 1: 0], P0 [1: 2: 2: 1], (K2, P2) 2 [2: 2: 1: 2] times, (C4B, K4, C4F) 4 [4: 4: 5: 5] times, (P2, K2) 2 [2: 2: 1: 2] times, P0 [1: 2: 2: 1], K0 [0: 1: 1: 0].
Row 8: As row 2.
These 8 rows form body patt.
Cont in patt until back meas 24 [25: 26: 27: 28] cm, ending with RS facing for next row.
Shape armholes
Keeping patt correct, cast off 2 sts at beg of next 2 rows. 60 [62: 66: 70: 74] sts.
Dec 1 st at each end of next and foll alt row. 56 [58: 62: 66: 70] sts.
Cont straight until armhole meas 14 [15: 16: 17: 18] cm, ending with RS facing for next row.
Shape shoulders and back neck
Next row (RS): Cast off 7 [7: 8: 9: 10] sts, patt until there are 11 [11: 12: 12: 13] sts on right needle and turn, leaving rem sts on a holder.
Work each side of neck separately.
Cast off 3 sts at beg of next row.
Cast off rem 8 [8: 9: 9: 10] sts.
With RS facing, rejoin yarn to rem sts, cast off centre 20 [22: 22: 24: 24] sts, patt to end.
Complete to match first side, reversing shapings.

FRONT
Work as given for back until 18 rows less have been worked than on back to beg of shoulder shaping, ending with RS facing for next row.
Divide for front opening
Next row (RS): Patt 26 [27: 29: 31: 33] sts and turn, leaving rem sts on a holder.
Work each side of neck separately.
Work 12 rows, ending with **WS** facing for next row.
Shape neck
Keeping patt correct, cast off 6 [7: 7: 8: 8] sts at beg of next row.

20 [20: 22: 23: 25] sts.

Dec 1 st at neck edge of next 4 rows, ending with RS facing for next row. 16 [16: 18: 19: 21] sts.

Shape shoulder

Cast off 7 [7: 8: 9: 10] sts at beg and dec 1 st at end of next row.

Work 1 row.

Cast off rem 8 [8: 9: 9: 10] sts.

With RS facing, rejoin yarn to rem sts, cast off centre 4 sts, patt to end.

Complete to match first side, reversing shapings.

SLEEVES

Using 6mm (US 10) needles cast on 33 [35: 37: 39: 41] sts.

Row 1 (RS): P0 [1: 0: 0: 0], K2 [2: 0: 1: 2], (P2, K2) 1 [1: 2: 2: 2] times, P3, (K3, P3) 3 times, (K2, P2) 1 [1: 2: 2: 2] times, K2 [2: 0: 1: 2], P0 [1: 0: 0: 0].

Row 2: K0 [1: 0: 0: 0], P2 [2: 0: 1: 2], (K2, P2) 1 [1: 2: 2: 2] times, K3, (P3, K3) 3 times, (P2, K2) 1 [1: 2: 2: 2] times, P2 [2: 0: 1: 2], K0 [1: 0: 0: 0]. These 2 rows form rib.

Work in rib for a further 10 rows, dec 1 st at centre of last row and ending with RS facing for next row. 32 [34: 36: 38: 40] sts.

Change to 7mm (US 10½) needles.

Beg and ending rows as indicated and repeating the 16 row patt rep throughout, now work in patt from chart as folls:

Inc 1 st at each end of 5th [5th: 7th: 7th: 9th] and every foll 6th [6th: 8th: 8th: 10th] row to 46 [40: 48: 42: 50] sts, then on every foll – [8th: 10th: 10th: 12th] row until there are – [48: 50: 52: 54] sts, taking inc sts into patt.

Cont straight until sleeve meas 31 [35: 39: 43: 47] cm, ending with RS facing for next row.

Shape top

Keeping patt correct, cast off 2 sts at beg of next 2 rows. 42 [44: 46: 48: 50] sts.

Dec 1 st at each end of next 2 rows, ending with RS facing for next

row.

Cast off rem 38 [40: 42: 44: 46] sts.

MAKING UP

Press as described on the information page.

Join both shoulder seams using back stitch, or mattress stitch if preferred.

Button band

With RS facing and using 6mm (US 10) needles, pick up and knit 15 sts along row-end edge of one side of front opening (left front for a girl, or right front for a boy), between base of opening and beg of neck shaping.

Row 1 (WS): P3, *K3, P3, rep from * to end.

Row 2: K3, *P3, K3, rep from * to end.

These 2 rows form rib.

Work in rib for a further 5 rows, ending with RS facing for next row. Cast off in rib.

Buttonhole band

With RS facing and using 6mm (US 10) needles, pick up and knit 15 sts along other row-end edge of front opening, between base of opening and beg of neck shaping.

Work in rib as given for button band for 3 rows, ending with RS facing for next row.

For a girl

Row 4 (RS): K3, P2tog tbl, yrn, rib 10.

For a boy

Row 4 (RS): Rib 10, yrn, P2tog, K3.

For a girl or a boy

Work in rib for a further 3 rows, ending with RS facing for next row. Cast off in rib.

Lay buttonhole band over button band and sew row-end edges to cast-off sts at base of front opening.

Collar

With RS facing and using 6mm (US 10) circular needle, beg and ending

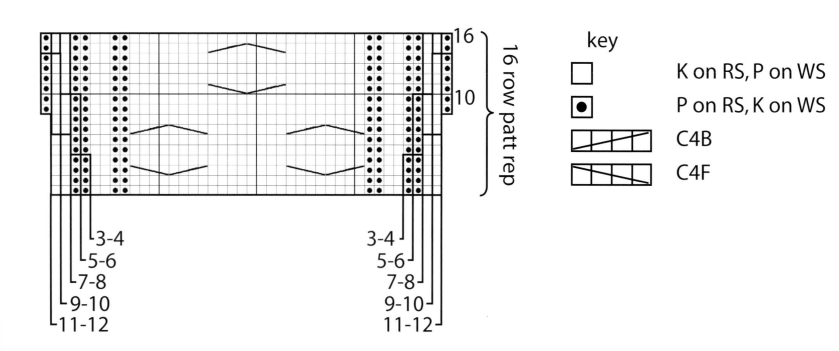

key

□ K on RS, P on WS

⊡ P on RS, K on WS

C4B

C4F

halfway across top of bands, pick up and knit 17 [19: 19: 19: 19] sts up right side of neck, 29 [31: 31: 31: 31] sts from back, then 17 [19: 19: 19: 19] sts down left side of neck. 63 [69: 69: 69: 69] sts.

Row 1 (RS of collar, WS of body): K3, ★P3, K3, rep from ★ to end.
This row sets position of rib as given for front bands.
Keeping rib correct, cont as folls:

Row 2: Rib 46 [50: 50: 50: 50], wrap next st (by slipping next st on left needle onto right needle, taking yarn to opposite side of work between needles and then slipping same st back onto left needle – when working back across wrapped sts, work the wrapped st and the wrapping loop tog as one st) and turn.

Row 3: Rib 29 [31: 31: 31: 31], wrap next st and turn.

Row 4: Rib 31 [33: 33: 33: 33], wrap next st and turn.

Row 5: Rib 33 [35: 35: 35: 35], wrap next st and turn.

Row 6: Rib 35 [37: 37: 37: 37], wrap next st and turn.

Row 7: Rib 37 [39: 39: 39: 39], wrap next st and turn.

Row 8: Rib 39 [41: 41: 41: 41], wrap next st and turn.

Row 9: Rib 41 [43: 43: 43: 43], wrap next st and turn.

Cont in this way, working 2 more sts on every row before wrapping next st and turning, until the foll row has been worked:

Next row: Rib 57 [63: 63: 63: 63], wrap next st and turn.

Next row: Rib to end.

Using a 7mm (US 10½) needle, cast off **loosely** in rib.

Sew row-end edges of collar to rem free row-end edges of front bands.

See information page for finishing instructions, setting in sleeves using the shallow set-in method.

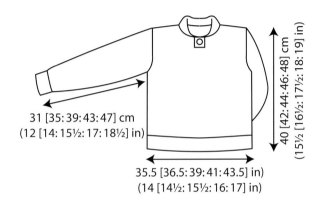

❖❖❖ Ella
By Marie Wallin

Main Image Page 33

SIZE
To fit age

| 5-6 | 7-8 | 9-10 | 11-12 | years |

YARN
Rowan Wool Cotton

| 8 | 9 | 9 | 10 | x 50gm |

(photographed in Ship Shape 955)

NEEDLES
1 pair 4mm (no 8) (US 6) needles

TENSION
21 sts and 41 rows to 10 cm measured over g st using 4mm (US 6) needles.

BACK and FRONT (both alike)
Using 4mm (US 6) needles cast on 84 [88: 92: 96] sts.
Work in g st for 12 cm, ending with RS facing for next row.
Dec 1 st at each end of next row. 82 [86: 90: 94] sts.
Cont straight until work meas 33 [34: 35: 36] cm, ending with RS facing for next row.

Shape for cap sleeves
Inc 1 st at each end of next and foll 4 alt rows, then on foll 4 rows, ending with **WS** facing for next row. 100 [104: 108: 112] sts.
Place markers at both ends of last row to denote base of armhole openings.
Cont straight until work meas 14 [15: 16: 17] cm from markers, ending with RS facing for next row.

Shape shoulders and funnel neck
Cast off 8 [8: 8: 9] sts at beg of next 2 [4: 6: 2] rows, then 7 [7: 7: 8] sts

at beg of foll 6 [4: 2: 6] rows. 42 [44: 46: 46] sts.
Dec 1 st at each end of next 3 rows, then on foll 2 alt rows.
32 [34: 36: 36] sts.
Work 6 rows, ending with **WS** facing for next row.
Cast off **loosely** knitwise (on **WS**).

MAKING UP
Press as described on the information page.
Join both shoulder and funnel neck seams using back stitch, or mattress
stitch if preferred.
Armhole borders (both alike)
With RS facing and using 4mm (US 6) needles, pick up and knit
58 [64: 68: 72] sts evenly along armhole edge between markers.
Work in g st for 8 cm, ending with RS of body facing for next row.
Cast off knitwise.
See information page for finishing instructions, reversing armhole
borders seam for last 5 cm. Fold 4 cm turn-back to RS and secure in
place to shoulder seam and at underarm.
Belt
Using 4mm (US 6) needles cast on 9 sts.
Work in g st for 100 cm.
Cast off.

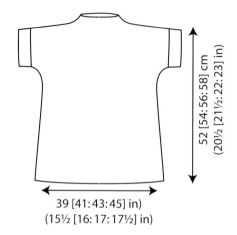

52 [54: 56: 58] cm
(20½ [21½: 22: 23] in)

39 [41: 43: 45] in)
(15½ [16: 17: 17½] in)

❖ ❖ **Charlie Snood**
By Lisa Richardson

Main Image Page 8 & 33

SIZE
One size

YARN
Rowan Cocoon
    2   x 100gm
(photographed in Scree 803 and Tundra 808)

NEEDLES
7mm (no 2) (US 10½) circular needle

TENSION
18 sts and 18½ rows to 10 cm measured over patt using 7mm (US 10½)
needles.

FINISHED SIZE
Completed snood measures 25 cm (10 ins) deep and is 62 cm (24½ ins)
all round.

SNOOD
Using 7mm (US 10½) needles cast on 112 sts.

Taking care not to twist cast-on edge and working in rounds, cont as
folls:
Round 1 (RS): ★P1, K1, rep from ★ to end.
Rounds 2 to 5: As round 1.
Now work in patt as folls:
Rounds 6 to 8: ★P5, K1, P1, K1, rep from ★ to end.
Round 9: ★Slip next 3 sts purlwise, K2tog, pass 3 slipped sts over, K1,
M1, inc twice in next st, M1, K1, rep from ★ to end.
Rounds 10 to 14: ★P1, K1, P5, K1, rep from ★ to end.
Round 15: ★M1, inc twice in next st, M1, K1, slip next 3 sts purlwise,
K2tog, pass 3 slipped sts over, K1, rep from ★ to end.
Rounds 16 and 17: ★P5, K1, P1, K1, rep from ★ to end.
Rounds 6 to 17 form patt.
Cont in patt until work meas 22 cm.
Now rep round 1, 5 times.
Cast off in rib.

MAKING UP
Press as described on the information page.

 Tobias

By Grace Melville

Main Image Page 8

SIZE

To fit age

| 3-4 | 5-6 | 7-8 | 9-10 | 11-12 | years |

YARN

Rowan British Sheep Breeds DK

A Brown Bluefaced Leicester 781

| 3 | 4 | 4 | 5 | 5 | x 50gm |

B Bluefaced Leicester 780

| 3 | 3 | 4 | 4 | 5 | x 50gm |

NEEDLES

1 pair 3¼mm (no 10) (US 3) needles
1 pair 4mm (no 8) (US 6) needles

TENSION

25 sts and 40 rows to 10 cm measured over patt using 4mm (US 6) needles.

Pattern note: When working patt, slip all sts purlwise with yarn at **RS** of work – this is front of work on RS rows, and back of work on WS rows.

BACK

Using 3¼mm (US 3) needles and yarn A cast on 81 [87: 89: 95: 99] sts.
Row 1 (RS): K1, *P1, K1, rep from * to end.
Row 2: P1, *K1, P1, rep from * to end.
These 2 rows form rib.
Work in rib for 1 row more, ending with **WS** facing for next row.
Row 4 (WS): Rib 5 [3: 2: 5: 1], M1, (rib 7 [8: 7: 7: 8], M1) 10 [10: 12: 12: 12] times, rib 6 [4: 3: 6: 2]. 92 [98: 102: 108: 112] sts.
Change to 4mm (US 6) needles.
Beg and ending rows as indicated, working chart row 1 **once only** and then repeating chart rows 2 to 29 **throughout**, now work in patt from chart as folls:
Cont straight until back meas 27 [28: 29: 30: 31] cm, ending with RS facing for next row.

Shape armholes

Keeping patt correct, cast off 3 sts at beg of next 2 rows. 86 [92: 96: 102: 106] sts.
Dec 1 st at each end of next and foll 4 alt rows. 76 [82: 86: 92: 96] sts.
Cont straight until armhole meas 13 [14: 15: 16: 17] cm, ending with

RS facing for next row.

Shape shoulders and back neck

Cast off 5 [6: 6: 7: 7] sts at beg of next 2 rows, then 5 [6: 6: 6: 7] sts at beg of foll 2 rows. 56 [58: 62: 66: 68] sts.
Next row (RS): Cast off 5 [5: 6: 6: 7] sts, patt until there are 8 [8: 8: 9: 9] sts on right needle and turn, leaving rem sts on a holder.
Work each side of neck separately.
Cast off 3 sts at beg of next row.
Cast off rem 5 [5: 5: 6: 6] sts.
With RS facing, rejoin appropriate yarn to rem sts, cast off centre 30 [32: 34: 36: 36] sts, patt to end.
Complete to match first side, reversing shapings.

FRONT

Work as given for back until 10 [10: 10: 12: 12] rows less have been worked than on back to beg of shoulder shaping, ending with RS facing for next row.

Shape neck

Next row (RS): Patt 28 [30: 31: 34: 36] sts and turn, leaving rem sts on a holder.
Work each side of neck separately.
Keeping patt correct, dec 1 st at neck edge of next 6 rows, then on foll 1 [1: 1: 2: 2] alt rows. 21 [23: 24: 26: 28] sts.
Work 1 row, ending with RS facing for next row.

Shape shoulder

Cast off 5 [6: 6: 7: 7] sts at beg and dec 1 st at end of next row.
Work 1 row.
Cast off 5 [6: 6: 6: 7] sts at beg of next row, then 5 [5: 6: 6: 7] sts at beg of foll alt row.
Work 1 row.
Cast off rem 5 [5: 5: 6: 6] sts.
With RS facing, rejoin appropriate yarn to rem sts, cast off centre 20 [22: 24: 24: 24] sts, patt to end.
Complete to match first side, reversing shapings.

SLEEVES

Using 3¼mm (US 3) needles and yarn A cast on 43 [45: 47: 49: 51] sts.
Work in rib as given for back for 3 rows, ending with **WS** facing for next row.
Row 4 (WS): Rib 3 [4: 5: 3: 4], M1, (rib 9 [9: 9: 7: 7], M1) 4 [4: 4: 6: 6] times, rib 4 [5: 6: 4: 5]. 48 [50: 52: 56: 58] sts.

Change to 4mm (US 6) needles.

Beg and ending rows as indicated, now work in patt from chart, shaping sides by inc 1 st at each end of 11th [11th: 11th: 13th: 13th] and every foll 12th [12th: 12th: 14th: 14th] row to 58 [58: 58: 66: 68] sts, then on every foll 14th [14th: 14th: 16th: 16th] row until there are 64 [68: 72: 76: 80] sts, taking inc sts into patt.

Cont straight until sleeve meas 31 [35: 39: 43: 47] cm, ending with RS facing for next row.

Shape top

Keeping patt correct, cast off 3 sts at beg of next 2 rows. 58 [62: 66: 70: 74] sts.

Dec 1 st at each end of next and foll 2 alt rows, then on foll row, ending with RS facing for next row.

Cast off rem 50 [54: 58: 62: 66] sts.

MAKING UP

Press as described on the information page.

Join right shoulder seam using back stitch, or mattress stitch if preferred.

Neckband

With RS facing, using 3¼mm (US 3) needles and yarn A, pick up and knit 10 [10: 10: 12: 12] sts down left side of neck, 19 [21: 23: 23: 23] sts from front, 10 [10: 10: 12: 12] sts up right side of neck, then 36 [38: 40: 42: 42] sts from back. 75 [79: 83: 89: 89] sts.

Beg with row 2, work in rib as given for back for 3 rows, ending with RS facing for next row.

Cast off in rib.

See information page for finishing instructions, setting in sleeves using the shallow set-in method.

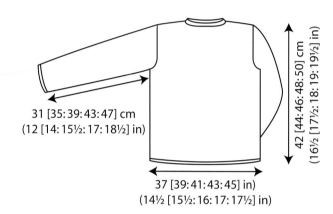

31 [35: 39: 43: 47] cm
(12 [14: 15½: 17: 18½] in)

42 [44: 46: 48: 50] cm
(16½ [17½: 18: 19: 19½] in)

37 [39: 41: 43: 45] in)
(14½ [15½: 16: 17: 17½] in)

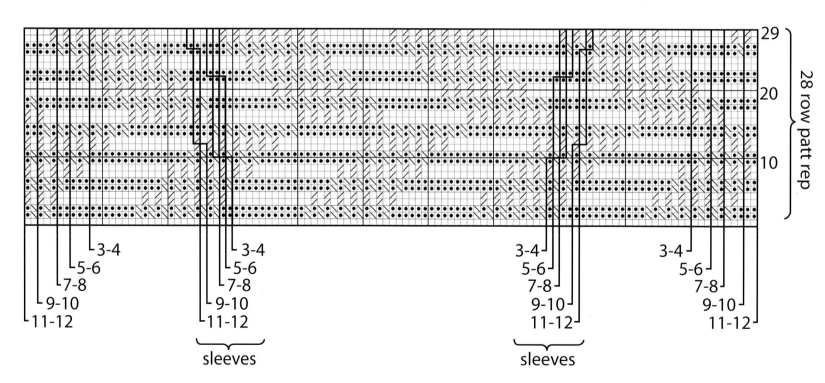

29

20

10

28 row patt rep

3-4
5-6
7-8
9-10
11-12

3-4
5-6
7-8
9-10
11-12

sleeves

3-4
5-6
7-8
9-10
11-12

3-4
5-6
7-8
9-10
11-12

sleeves

key

☐ using yarn A, P on RS, K on WS

▨ using yarn A, slip 1

⊡ using yarn B, P on RS, K on WS

◨ using yarn B, slip 1

TENSION

Obtaining the correct tension is perhaps the single factor which can make the difference between a successful garment and a disastrous one. It controls both the shape and size of an article, so any variation, however slight, can distort the finished garment.

Different designers feature in our books and it is their tension, given at the start of each pattern, which you must match. We recommend that you knit a square in pattern and/or stocking stitch (depending on the pattern instructions) of perhaps 5 - 10 more stitches and 5 - 10 more rows than those given in the tension note. Mark out the central 10cm square with pins. If you have too many stitches to 10cm try again using thicker needles, if you have too few stitches to 10cm try again using finer needles. Once you have achieved the correct tension your garment will be knitted to the measurements indicated in the size diagram shown at the end of the pattern.

SIZING & SIZE DIAGRAM NOTE

The instructions are given for the smallest size. Where they vary, work the figures in brackets for the larger sizes. One set of figures refers to all sizes. Included with most patterns in this magazine is a 'size diagram', of the finished garment and its dimensions. The measurement shown at the bottom of each 'size diagram' shows the garment width 2.5cm below the armhole shaping.

CHART NOTE

Many of the patterns in the book are worked from charts. Each square on a chart represents a stitch and each line of squares a row of knitting. Each colour used is given a different letter and these are shown in the materials section, or in the key alongside the chart of each pattern. When working from the charts, read odd rows (K) from right to left and even rows (P) from left to right, unless otherwise stated. When working lace from a chart it is important to note that all but the largest size may have to alter the first and last few stitches in order not to lose or gain stitches over the row.

WORKING A LACE PATTERN

When working a lace pattern it is important to remember that if you are unable to work both the increase and corresponding decrease and vica versa, the stitches should be worked in stocking stitch.

KNITTING WITH COLOUR

There are two main methods of working colour into a knitted fabric: Intarsia and Fairisle techniques. The first method produces a single thickness of fabric and is usually used where a colour is only required in a particular area of a row and does not form a repeating pattern across the row, as in the fairisle technique.

Intarsia: The simplest way to do this is to cut short lengths of yarn for each motif or block of colour used in a row. Then joining in the various colours at the appropriate point on the row, link one colour to the next by twisting them around each other where they meet on the wrong side to avoid gaps. All ends can then either be darned along the colour join lines, as each motif is completed or then can be "knitted-in" to the fabric of the knitting as each colour is worked into the pattern. This is done in much the same way as

"weaving- in" yarns when working the Fairisle technique and does save time darning-in ends. It is essential that the tension is noted for Intarsia as this may vary from the stocking stitch if both are used in the same pattern.

Fairisle type knitting: When two or three colours are worked repeatedly across a row, strand the yarn not in use loosely behind the stitches being worked. If you are working with more than two colours, treat the "floating" yarns as if they were one yarn and always spread the stitches to their correct width to keep them elastic. It is advisable not to carry the stranded or "floating" yarns over more than three stitches at a time, but to weave them under and over the colour you are working. The "floating" yarns are therefore caught at the back of the work.

FINISHING INSTRUCTIONS

After working for hours knitting a garment, it seems a great pity that many garments are spoiled because such little care is taken in the pressing and finishing process. Follow the text below for a truly professional-looking garment.

PRESSING

Block out each piece of knitting and following the instructions on the ball band press the garment pieces, omitting the ribs. Tip: Take special care to press the edges, as this will make sewing up both easier and neater. If the ball band indicates that the fabric is not to be pressed, then covering the blocked out fabric with a damp white cotton cloth and leaving it to stand will have the desired effect. Darn in all ends neatly along the selvage edge or a colour join, as appropriate.

STITCHING

When stitching the pieces together, remember to match areas of colour and texture very carefully where they meet. Use a seam stitch such as back stitch or mattress stitch for all main knitting seams and join all ribs and neckband with mattress stitch, unless otherwise stated.

CONSTRUCTION

Having completed the pattern instructions, join left shoulder and neckband seams as detailed above. Sew the top of the sleeve to the body of the garment using the method detailed in the pattern, referring to the appropriate guide:

Straight cast-off sleeves: Place centre of cast-off edge of sleeve to shoulder seam. Sew top of sleeve to body, using markers as guidelines where applicable.

Square set-in sleeves: Place centre of cast-off edge of sleeve to shoulder seam. Set sleeve head into armhole, the straight sides at top of sleeve to form a neat right-angle to cast-off sts at armhole on back and front.

Shallow set-in sleeves: Place centre of cast off edge of sleeve to shoulder seam. Match decreases at beg of armhole shaping to decreases at top of sleeve. Sew sleeve head into armhole, easing in shapings.

Set- in sleeves: Place centre of cast-off edge of sleeve to shoulder seam. Set in sleeve, easing sleeve head into armhole.

Join side and sleeve seams. Slip stitch pocket edgings and linings into place. Sew on buttons to correspond with buttonholes. Ribbed welts and neckbands and any areas of garter stitch should not be pressed.

Information

ABBREVIATIONS

K	knit
P	purl
st(s)	stitch(es)
inc	increas(e)(ing)
dec	decreas(e)(ing)
st st	stocking stitch (1 row K , 1 row P)
g st	garter stitch (K every row)
beg	begin(ning)
foll	following
rem	remain(ing)
rev st st	reverse stocking stitch (1 row K , 1 row P)
rep	repeat
alt	alternate
cont	continue
patt	pattern
tog	together
mm	millimetres
cm	centimetres
in(s)	inch(es)
RS	right side
WS	wrong side
sl 1	slip one stitch
psso	pass slipped stitch over

p2sso	pass 2 slipped stitches over
tbl	through back of loop
M1	make one stitch by picking up horizontal loop before next stitch and knitting into back of it
M1P	make one stitch by picking up horizontal loop before next stitch and purling into back of it
yfwd	yarn forward
yrn	yarn round needle
meas	measures
0	no stitches, times or rows
-	no stitches, times or rows for that size
yon	yarn over needle
yfrn	yarn forward round needle
wyib	with yarn at back

Crochet Terms

UK crochet terms and abbreviations have been used throughout. The list below gives the US equivalent below where they vary.

Abbrev.	UK	US
dc	double crochet	single crochet
htr	half treble	half double crochet
tr	treble	double crochet

EXPERIENCE RATING

Easy, straight forward knitting	Suitable for the average knitter	For the more experienced knitter

When you knit a Rowan baby or children's design, we want you to be happy with the look and feel of the finished garment. This all starts with the size and fit of the design you choose. To help you to achieve the correct fit for your baby or child, we have looked at the sizing of our baby and children's patterns.

This has resulted in the introduction of the sizing chart below. Dimensions in the chart below are body measurements, not garment dimensions, therefore please refer to the measuring guide to help you to determine which is the best size for your baby or child.

MEASURING GUIDE

For maximum comfort and to ensure the correct fit when choosing the size to knit, please follow the tips below when checking the size of your baby or child.

Measure your baby or child gently, close to the body over their underwear, but don't pull the tape measure too tight!

- **Height** – measure from the top of your baby's or child head to their feet when they are laying or standing straight.

- **Chest** – measure around the fullest part of the chest and across the shoulder blades.

- **Waist** – measure around the natural waistline just above the hip bone.

- **Hips** – measure around the fullest part of the bottom.

If you don't wish to measure your baby or child, note the size of their or your favourite jumper that you like the fit of. Our sizes are comparable to the clothing sizes from the major high street retailers, so if the favourite jumper is 6 months or 3 years, then our 6 months or 3 years size should measure approximately the same. Measure this favourite jumper and compare the measurements against the size diagram at the end of the pattern you wish to knit.

Finally, once you have decided which size is best for you to knit, please ensure that you achieve the correct tension for the design you are planning to knit.

Remember if your tension is too loose, your garment will be bigger than the pattern size and you may use more yarn. If your tension is too tight, your garment will be smaller than the pattern size and you may have yarn left over. Furthermore if your tension is incorrect, the handle of your fabric will be either too stiff or too floppy and will not fit properly. As you invest money and time in knitting one of our designs, it really does make sense to check your tension before starting your project.

STANDARD SIZING GUIDE FOR CHILDREN

AGE	3–4yrs	5–6yrs	7–8 yrs	9–10 yrs	11–12 yrs	
To fit height	38.5 – 41	43.25 – 45.5	48 – 50.25	52.75 – 55	57.5 – 60	inches
	98 – 104	110 – 116	122 – 128	134 – 140	146 – 152	cm
To fit chest	21.75 – 22.5	23 – 24	25 – 26.5	27 – 28.75	29.5 – 31	inches
	55 – 57	59 – 61	63 – 67	69 – 73	75 – 79	cm
To fit waist	20.75 – 21.25	21.5 – 22.25	23 – 23.75	24 – 25	25.25 – 26.25	inches
	53 – 54	55 – 57	58 – 60	61 – 64	64 – 67	cm
To fit hips	22.75 – 23	24.5 – 25.5	26.75 – 28	28.75 – 30.75	31.5 – 32.5	inches
	58 – 60	62 – 65	68 – 71	73 – 78	80 – 83	cm

Stockist

AUSTRALIA: Australian Country Spinners Pty Ltd, Level 7, 409 St. Kilda Road, Melbourne 3004. Tel: 03 9380 3830 Email: tkohut@auspinners.com.au

AUSTRIA: Coats Harlander GmbH, Autokaderstrasse 31, Wien A –1210. Tel: (01) 27716

BELGIUM: Coats Benelux, Ring Oost 14A, Ninove, 9400 Tel: 054 318989 Email: sales.coatsninove@coats.com

CANADA: Westminster Fibers, 8 Shelter Drive, Greer, South Carolina, 29650 Tel: 800 445-9276 Email: info@westminsterfibers.com Web: www.westminsterfibers.com

CHINA: Coats Shanghai Ltd, No 9 Building , Baosheng Road, Songjiang Industrial Zone, Shanghai. Tel: 86 21 5774 3733 Email: victor.li@coats.com

DENMARK: Coats HP A/S, Tagensvej 85C, St.tv., Copenhagen Tel: 45 35 86 90 49

FINLAND: Coats Opti Crafts Oy, Ketjutie 3, Kerava , 04220 Tel: (358) 9 274871 Email: coatsopti@coats.com Web: wwwcoatscrafts.fi

FRANCE: Coats Steiner, 100 Avenue du Général de Gaulle, Mehun-Sur-Yèvre, 18500 Tel: 02 48 23 12 30 Web: www.coatscrafts.fr

GERMANY: Coats GmbH, Kaiserstrasse 1, Kenzingen, 79341 Tel: 07162-14346 Web: www.coatsgmbh.de

HOLLAND: Coats Benelux, Ring Oost 14A, Ninove, 9400, Belgium Tel: 0346 35 37 00 Email: sales.coatsninove@coats.com

HONG KONG: Coats Shanghai Ltd, No 8 Building , Export & Processing Garden, Songjiang Industrial Zone, Shanghai, China. Tel: (86- 21) 57743733-326 Email: victor.li@coats.com

ICELAND: Rowan At Storkurinn, Laugavegur 59, Reykjavik, 101 Tel: 551 8258 Email: storkurinn@simnet.is Web: www.storkurinn.is

ISRAEL: Beit Hasidkit, Ms. Offra Tzenger, Sokolov St No 2, Kfar Sava, 44256 Tel: (972) 9 7482381

ITALY: Coats cucirini srl, Viale sarca no 223, Milano, 20126

KOREA: Coats Korea Co. Lt, 5F Eyeon B/D, 935-40 Bangbae-Dong, Seocho-Gu, Seoul, 137-060 Tel: 82-2-521-6262 Web: www.coatskorea.co.kr

LEBANON: y.knot, Saifi Village, Mkhalissiya Street 162, Beirut Tel: (961) 1 992211 Email: y.knot@cyberia.net.lb

LUXEMBOURG: Coats Benelux, Ring Oost 14A, Ninove, 9400, Belgium Tel: 0346 35 37 00 Email: sales.coatsninove@coats.com

MALTA: John Gregory Ltd, 8 Ta'Xbiex Sea Front, Msida, MSD 1512, Malta Tel: +356 2133 0202 Email: raygreg@onvol.net

NEW ZEALAND: ACS New Zealand, 1 March Place, Belfast, Christchurch Tel: 64-3-323-6665

NORWAY: Coats Knappehuset AS, Pb 100, Ulset, Bergen, 5873 Tel: 55 53 93 00

PORTUGAL: Coats & Clark, Quinta de Cravel, Apartado 444, Vila Nova de Gaia 4431-968 Tel: 223770700 Web: www.crafts.com.pt

SINGAPORE: Golden Dragon Store, 101 Upper Cross Street, #02-51, People's Park Centre, 058357, Singapore Tel: (65) 65358454/65358234 Email: gdscraft@hotmail.com

SOUTH AFRICA: Arthur Bales Ltd, 62 Fourth Avenue, Linden, Johannesburg, 2195 Tel: (27) 118 882 401 Email: arthurb@new.co.za Web: www.arthurbales.co.za

SPAIN: Coats Fabra, SA, Santa Adria, 20, Barcelona, 08030 Tel: (34) 93 290 84 00 Email: atencion.clientes@coats.com Web: www.coatscrafts.es

SWEDEN: Coats Expotex AB, JA Wettergrensgata 7, Vastra Frolunda, Goteborg, 431 30 Tel: (46) 33 720 79 00

SWITZERLAND: Coats Stroppel AG, Turgi (AG), CH-5300 Tel: 056 298 12 20

TAIWAN: Cactus Quality Co Ltd, 7FL-2, No. 140, Sec. 2 Roosevelt Road, Taipei, Taiwan, R.O.C. 10084 Tel: 00886-2-23656527 Email:cqcl@ms17.hinet.net Web: www.excelcraft.com.tw

THAILAND: Global Wide Trading, 10 Lad Prao Soi 88, Bangkok 10310 Tel: 00 662 933 9019 Email: TheNeedleWorld@yahoo.com – global.wide@yahoo.com

U.S.A.: Westminster Fibers Inc, 8 Shelter Drive, Greer, 29650, South Carolina Tel: (800) 445-9276 Email: info@westminsterfibers.com Web: www.westminsterfibers.com

U.K: Rowan, Green Lane Mill, Holmfirth, West Yorkshire, England HD9 2DX Tel: +44 (0) 1484 681881 Email: mail@knitrowan.com Web: www.knitrowan.com

For stockists in all other countries please contact Rowan for details